BRENT LIBRARIES

Please return/renew this item
by the last date shown.
Books may also be renewed by
phone or online.
Tel: 0115 929 3388
On-line www.brent.gov.uk/libraryservice

Dedication

I dedicate this book to Zara, my wonderful and intrepid daughter, with heartfelt thanks for her loving support, interesting challenges and constant inspiration.

Also to all the heroines and heroes who keep battling valiantly with the stresses of life. It is my hope that this book will provide some new tools and new perspectives to make the path less difficult and more joyful for everyone.

Stress Control
Stress-Busting Strategies for the 21st Century

Author

Susan Balfour

Published by:

Anshan Ltd
6 Newlands Road
Tunbridge Wells
Kent. TN4 9AT

Tel: +44 (0) 1892 557767
Fax: +44 (0) 1892 530358

e-mail: info@anshan.co.uk
website: www.anshan.co.uk

© 2013 Anshan Ltd

ISBN: 978 1 848290 62 4

This book is a completely revised and updated version of *Release your Stress* (ISBN 0 340 78588 8) published in 2002 by Hodder and Stoughton, London.

British Library Cataloguing in Publication Data

A catalogue record for this book is available from the British Library.

Copy Editor: Catherine Lain

Illustrator: Leigh East

Cover Design: Emma Randall

Cover Image: Shutterstock

Typeset by: Kerry Press, Luton, Bedfordshire

Contents

List of figures, exercises and case studies

Figures

Exercises

Case studies

Acknowledgements

There are so many friends and colleagues to whom I owe grateful thanks for their support and encouragement whilst I journeyed through the bumpy terrain of writing this book. Firstly, I should like to express my gratitude to my literary agent, Charlotte Howard, for her constant support and helpful suggestions. Affectionate thanks and enormous appreciation go to Amber Lloyd, founder of the Relaxation for Living Charity that has helped and supported thousands of people suffering from tension, stress, panic attacks, hyperventilation and other symptoms of the stress syndrome. I am greatly appreciative of the knowledge and skills that she taught me, and that I use in my life and work every day – most of which are included in this book. She was a true pioneer in the teaching of stress management and the importance of relaxation. Another pioneer I should like to acknowledge is the late Betty Parsons, who helped so many mothers-to-be with her wisdom and humour and unique teaching of relaxation techniques, and with whom I was privileged to train alongside at the Centre for Transpersonal Psychology.

I am also deeply indebted to Barbara Somers and the late Ian Gordon-Brown for their wonderful training in Transpersonal Psychology, and for their outstanding example of 'walking the talk'. Much inspirational work is continuing to flow into the world as a result of their wisdom and generosity of spirit. I should also like to acknowledge with appreciation the work of Dr Peter Nixon, who pioneered sleep therapy in the management of heart disease and who recognised the importance of understanding the stresses people faced that lead to coronary dysfunction. I have drawn on his work for my own practice, especially his insights into hyperventilation syndrome. I thank Mrs Susan Nixon for giving permission for me to use his Human Function Curve diagram (figure 4). I appreciate with gratitude all those who have paved the way towards the better knowledge we have today; we all stand on the shoulders of others.

I also thank my publishers, Shan and Andrew White, at Anshan Books for having faith in me, and I especially want to thank my editor, Catherine Lain, who has been wonderfully supportive and sensitive in her editing. Many thanks also to Leigh East for her excellent illustrations to the text. Loving thanks are due to my daughter, Zara, for her understanding support and insightful comments, as well as providing 'techy' help when my abilities in that area fail. My dear friend, Richard Marett, took me away from the keyboard at just the right moments for revitalising dinners, as did my great friend Diana Haydon – and how grateful I am for those interludes. My wonderful brother, John Pickett, is always a much appreciated 'sounding board' when I'm at my wits' end, as is John Clifton – huge thanks to both of you for being there when I need you. Another much valued friend, Philippa Steel, miraculously arrives with uplifting and sustaining bottles of champagne just when needed. Susie Trotter-Landry is a constant support providing beautiful country escapes, and Lee Sturgeon-Day inspires me with her pithy comments and her spiritual perspective. I am so fortunate to have many inspiring, supportive and wonderful friends and I thank and love you all.

Figure Acknowledgements

Figs. 1 and 2: © Wendy Chalmers Mill, from *RSI: Repetitive Strain Injury*, 1994, HarperCollins. Diagrams reproduced with kind permission of Wendy Chalmers Mill, ergonomics expert, corporate coach and NLP practitioner at: www.Positive-Performance.com. (See Useful Addresses.)

Fig. 4: © Dr P. G. F. Nixon. Reprinted with kind permission from Susan Nixon.

About the author

Susan Balfour is a psychotherapist who has made a special study of the stress syndrome: what causes stress reactions, how it affects our health and how to manage it in daily living. For over twenty years she has been teaching people how to understand their stress triggers, how to achieve a new perspective and how to unwind, relax and release themselves from tension and stress. She has a private therapy practice in southwest London where she sees individuals and couples for psychotherapy, counselling and stress management therapy; she also runs relaxation and stress management groups and seminars for companies, organisations, community groups and health professionals. She lectures extensively on the subject of stress management and self-management.

Companies Susan has worked with include: Barclays Bank, The London Business School, The British Council, The Royal College of Music, St. Bartholomew's Hospital, The Royal Free Hospital, The International Stress and Tension in Performance Society (ISTIP), Goldsmith's College, The Arts Centre Group, MIND mental health charity, Camden Neighbourhood Centre, as well as many other community, health, business and arts organisations.

Susan has been featured on a number of television programmes about stress and anxiety management. In addition she has worked with leading medical specialists on the management of Repetitive Strain Injury (RSI), also known as Upper Limb Disorder, as experienced by musicians and others engaged in repetitive movements, as well as office workers. She is the author of four books on stress

management, including being the major contributing expert to the Reader's Digest book: *Stay Calm, Stay Healthy.* She has produced and recorded a relaxation and stress control CD, entitled *Release Your Stress*, which is available to purchase from her website: www.releaseyourstress.co.uk
or by emailing susanbalfour@releaseyourstress.co.uk.

Introduction

In today's world we are becoming overwhelmed and overloaded by the very inventions that were supposed to enhance our quality of life; by the myriad wonders we have created for ourselves. We now have so many choices, possibilities, optional extras and adornments to the basic processes of living, that, far from providing the promised freedoms and utopias, they are tending to weigh us down and clutter us up, often causing more problems than they solve and increasing the stress of life at every level.

Many books have been written on the subject of stress over the past decade. Some of these have been heavy, academic and loaded with medical jargon, while others have been lighter, sometimes superficial in approach. I believe, however, that another kind of book is needed that views stress from a slightly different perspective; one that incorporates the old knowledge, but also looks at the subject with fresh eyes. It is time to question our preconceived ideas, and in these pages I shall put before you some alternative ways of approaching and thinking about life and its constant challenges.

We have different expectations in today's world and new needs in order to achieve a sense of well-being and contentment. Our awareness of ourselves, our fellow human beings and the planet we inhabit (not to mention the universe!) is changing almost daily due to the rapid advances in science, psychology, medicine and information technology. Alongside their benefits, these developments tend to throw up new problems with which to grapple. In many ways the goalposts have moved radically in the last few years.

Previously, stress was seen as a phenomenon that only happened to certain people in certain extreme situations. Now we have to recognise that stress is an integral part of the current culture of humankind and it affects all of us in one way or another. Stress is impacting on us as never before, and creates much discomfort and unease for almost everyone on the planet, in every different culture and at every level of society. We can no longer ignore the evidence that we are creating an environment that is none too 'human being-friendly', but equally we cannot go backwards or easily undo what is already created. Therefore, we need to find new approaches and new strategies for living alongside the stresses of the modern world.

Stress Control combines relevant medical information with physiological facts about the effects of stress on our bodily systems and also its psychological impact, in addition to offering a contemporary take on today's society. I shall bring together the best solutions from ancient wisdom teachings translated into useful concepts and procedures for current living, as well as new perspectives on the best modern ideas.

It is important that we understand more clearly what is happening to humankind at this point in the twenty-first century. But a further dimension is also needed: an inspiring and creative vision for the future, for how it could be, for how we *could* make it. In order to create a better future, it is imperative that we are not bogged down or weakened by too much stress today; we need strategies that release us to be creative, to use our full potential and to enjoy our lives. These are what I shall attempt to give you throughout this book and I will endeavour to inspire you towards greater fulfilment, both now and in your vision for your future.

Contrary to what many of us may hope, the problems and dilemmas of the complicated lifestyles we lead are not going to be resolved very easily and they definitely won't be taken care of by someone else! Therefore, we need to find new ways to deal with the stressors and pressures that are the inevitable result of our multi-layered lives, overloaded by endless media, too much information, incessant communication, more choice than we can comfortably handle, intense commercial pressure to have more possessions, be more successful, more good-looking, more slender and smarter than our peers. This is not to mention the stress of daily threats to our well-being from contaminated food, polluted atmospheres and powerful new strains of bacteria, along with the potential environmental dangers we have set up for ourselves in terms of climate change and the consequences of destroying our rainforests.

Overload has become a major stress for many of us. Too much crowding in our minds and nervous systems on a daily basis severely challenges our ability to cope. One of the obvious solutions to 'overload' is to 'offload', and in my view, an important part of controlling our stress levels is to begin re-assessing how much of the 'stuff' on our current agenda is truly helpful, life-enhancing and needed on our journey in the twenty-first century. Which aspects can we actually safely relegate to the metaphorical trash can or shredder? This can be approached as a kind of mammoth spring-clean where we chuck out all the unnecessary clutter and excess baggage we've been accumulating, often unconsciously, at every level of our lives. It needs to happen both at an individual, personal level, and on a collective global level; there is so much that we could discard as hindering our attempts at being happy and stress-free. Successful stress management is, fundamentally, about making the right choices.

That is what this book is about. I shall assist you in carrying out an audit of your life on many levels to help you discover what is weighing you down and holding you back, rather than being truly helpful and supportive to your life goals. Every dwelling place needs to be cleared out on a regular basis in order that the occupants can function in a relaxed and effective fashion. If you are constantly tripping over the clutter, or cannot find things buried deep in the chaos, you become tense and stressed, angry and panicky. Isn't this the state in which many of us find ourselves quite frequently? And, of course, it is just as essential to clear out the dwelling place of our thoughts and feelings, our inner self, and to address the mental clutter which may no longer be useful to us.

It is possible to sidestep or offload much of our stress by changing the way we look at it, or the way we go into action. These are two major themes I shall expand upon throughout the book. I shall be offering suggestions for new ways to tackle various different life areas and find new perspectives on old problems.

Changing our habits isn't easy, but I think it can be helpful to see that change is really simply a development, and development is inevitable in our lives. Just as a bud must develop into a flower or a leaf, and an acorn must develop into an oak tree, so too must we develop and change if we do not wish to stagnate or regress. Nothing in nature stands still and we too must develop or degenerate. John F. Kennedy put it like this:

'You cannot become what you want to be by remaining what you are.'

I see life as a constant process of transformation, from one developmental stage to the next, and I think humankind currently stands on the brink of a critical new step in its development. I believe that many of the stresses we face and many of today's difficult world events are offering us a challenge to change and transform, to rethink our values and objectives. I believe we are being challenged to grow and mature as individuals, societies and nations. We are being stressed into the realisation that we are interdependent and that all actions ripple out to affect the whole of humanity: we have to take account of each other. We cannot act unilaterally or selfishly anymore, for we are so completely linked-up around the globe that there is always a knock-on effect – a domino effect that, one way or another, will eventually ripple back to impact upon the place from which it originated.

This thought may seem a little daunting, but the positive aspect is that if we do the right things, then the right things will rebound back at us. I truly believe that we have a serious challenge in front of us and that it can be life-enhancing if we approach it in the right spirit. Many people agree that much needs changing around the globe, but the place to start this change is within ourselves and in our own lives, right here, right now. This book is offered as a starting point, as a combination of guide book, reference book and supportive and inspirational companion as you develop positive stress management strategies that will give you more control over your life, that will free your potential, your creativity and your energy for more enjoyment and fulfilment. Then perhaps you can help others do the same.

After more than twenty years of helping people to live in a better relationship with the stresses of life, I have come to certain conclusions and developed my own ideas and strategies for getting through with the least strain and the most joy, and I want to share these with you. Each chapter will address an aspect of daily life, look at why we become stressed by it, or bogged down in it, and then suggest ways to release ourselves, by taking a different approach, by rethinking the habitual and finding new perspectives, or by finding new ways to apply the old truths. We have to be inventive and creative – this is what we were born to be – and the more we apply our creativity the more fulfilled we will feel, and the less stressed.

Chapter 1

What's going on?

Stress has many causes, and stress can arise from any aspect of our lives, as well as being generated internally from our thoughts and feelings. We all have definitions as to what exactly constitutes stress. Some people maintain that stress is good for us as it keeps us focused and productive. Others advise that we avoid stress at all costs if we want to be happy. As we proceed through this book I shall endeavour to address all the differing views on stress; I shall define stress in specific ways and in specific situations, and help you to understand more about how and why stress affects you physically, emotionally and mentally. But most importantly of all I shall present you with strategies for releasing yourself from its grip, and for controlling its effect on your life.

However we define stress, I believe there is a need to take a new look at this phenomenon, for there can be no doubt that we all feel increasingly stressed by much of our modern world. In my view it is not going to get any better as we advance into the next few decades. In fact, I am convinced that the levels of stress will increase for quite a while. Or at least, the 'triggers' to stress will increase. It is up to each of us to ensure that we do not succumb, and that is what this book is about.

We are going to need new strategies with which to redesign our lives, perhaps to rethink many of our basic assumptions and to develop a new game plan, a new philosophy even, for a new era. Many people are already looking for alternatives and new perspectives in complementary medicine, in the rediscovery of ancient wisdoms, in retreats or taking holidays off the beaten track, as well as rethinking their career paths. There is almost a new consciousness beginning to unfold as the century progresses.

The stress of change

Part of the stress being experienced at any moment in history comes from the tension generated by change, by the old order of things having to give way to new ideas and practices. This of course happens globally, as well as in the smaller arena of our own personal lives. Stress is the adaptation, or adjustment, that is demanded of our mind and body to any changing circumstances, whether the change is physical, psychological or emotional. Change is demanding and tiring because we have to give a higher level of attention to new things, and this greater attention requires more energy than we use when just coasting along habitually. Of course, change can be stimulating and interesting, but too much change in too short a space of time can be overwhelming and exhausting. The more extreme the adjustment required, the more likely we are to experience stress and possibly distress.

Part of the reason that stress and anxiety are impacting more profoundly and widely today than ever before is the increasing speed with which new innovations are overtaking the old, and the huge demand this makes on all of us to adapt rapidly and frequently. On top of this demand to adjust our thinking, our practices and sometimes our priorities, there is now an additional demand for everything to happen faster than ever before and for each moment to be filled more completely.

We expect to cram more and more achievement into each day. This puts enormous pressure on us and on our coping ability. Our mental, emotional and physical resources are being stretched unceasingly, even though we may not always realise it from day-to-day. We may know in a vaguely abstract way that this is the case, but in my view we don't really give enough serious thought to just what is happening to us at this point in the twenty-first century. It often means that we don't take enough counter-measures, and I shall be addressing the important aspect of counterbalancing our stressors throughout the book. Stress tends to creep up on us in an accumulative manner. We adjust without quite realising what a strain it is to be confronted with relentless demands to absorb and react to high-speed news, views and innovation all around the clock, not to mention keeping up-to-date with all our friends' news and activities on social networking sites.

Whether we realise it or not, this pressure to keep up-to-date is impacting profoundly on most of us for most of the time. I see the results constantly in my therapy practice; people suffering from exhaustion, burnout, panic attacks, anxiety, hypertension and a whole host of other symptoms.

I think many people would agree that there is a general unease about the fact that we don't seem to feel as good as we think we should. A lot of advertising slogans emphasise 'peace of mind' as one of their benefits, yet peace of mind seems somewhat elusive in our current world. In fact, levels of anxiety, depression and mental ill health are rising, even among children. Today's lifestyle is not exactly producing the freedoms and happiness that we were implicitly promised by the new technologies and so-called labour-saving devices.

People who come to consult with me tell me they feel overloaded and overstretched, and somehow unfulfilled in important aspects of themselves. There is also a widespread feeling among many that they can't control their agendas sufficiently in order to create more time for what they really want to do. These are issues we shall be addressing as we proceed through the book. I shall analyse why we feel as we do, then offer you ideas and strategies for counteracting a lot of the pressures, as well as suggesting ways to take more control of your agenda to free up time for yourself and to bring about more positive changes.

Daydreaming time is important

A theme I hear constantly is that people have little energy and suffer from 'tired-all-the-time' syndrome, always feeling under pressure to keep on doing things, whilst not understanding quite how or why they have found themselves in this scenario. They say they feel driven by the multitude of tasks always needing their attention and panicky at not finding the time to step back, take an overview and work out a way of changing the situation. My clients tell me there never seems to be enough room in their schedule to take some time out for themselves, to relax or daydream to restore their energy. This is important because so-called daydreaming, or 'pottering about' time, is essential for rebalancing ourselves and connecting into the right hemisphere of the brain, from which arises much of our creativity and best ideas. Also, total relaxation of body and mind is one of the most effective counterbalances to overloading and excessive demands; deep relaxation restores depleted energy at all levels: mentally, physically and emotionally. It is a technique I teach to all my clients as an indispensable tool in their stress control strategy, and I will teach it to you in Chapter 9.

Limited adaptation energy

We tend to adjust to new circumstances without realising what is happening because we are very adaptable beings. But we need to take stock from time to time; to step back and try to look objectively at our situation and reassess if we are living in a way that is right for us. We can cope with extra demands and high pressure for a while – but not as a constant way of life. If you are continually being loaded up with more and more to adapt and adjust to, without sufficient resting time in-between, there comes a point when you will just collapse, possibly experiencing some health problem or a feeling of total burnout from unrelenting demands, with no energy to cope with anything.

Change of any kind, even pleasant change, is stressful because human beings actually have a limited amount of adaptive capacity; it is different for each of us, but if we are pushed beyond our individual limit we find it hard to cope. It is often difficult to admit to ourselves that we have limits, but the truth is that we do! We deny this fact at our peril: it may be a long time before it catches up with us, but eventually it will. The people most at risk from stress-related symptoms are those who never relax, never really switch off; those who are not willing to admit to themselves (or anyone else for that matter) that they feel tired, or that for the time being they have reached their limit. It is not a question of being an under-achiever, it is a question of balance, and in my experience the most successful people have almost always developed ways of switching off. I shall address this more fully in Chapter 7, but for the moment let's stay with the subject of change.

It is interesting to note that demanding life changes often cluster at the same time. Events like moving house, changing jobs or having a baby may coincide with divorce or redundancy, or the death of an aged parent may occur at the same time as our own retirement or as children leave home. Stressful life events superimpose themselves on all the other aspects of change in the world around us. And because we do not have unlimited adaptive resources, it is imperative that we take extra care of ourselves when we are dealing with a greater than usual number of life changes. This fact is well documented in the medical literature, but it is not sufficiently well-explained to the lay public, even by their doctors.

Below is a list of the most demanding life events you can experience, with a numerical value against each one. It is based on research carried out in the 1970s by doctors Thomas Holmes and Richard Rahe of the University of Washington School of Medicine, and is largely undisputed by subsequent studies. According to their findings, a score of 150 based on life events which have happened to you in the previous twelve month period, make your chances of developing an illness or health change roughly 50–50. If you score 300 points or over within the year, your chances of experiencing a health change rise to almost 90% as you have reached the danger zone as far as your body's adaptive capacity is concerned. This means that your body's resilience to combat disease or maintain its homeostasis (constant state of internal systems) will be severely taxed. For good health and emotional happiness try not to rise above a score of 150 points in any one year.

Obviously, it would be best to keep most years well below even that figure. If you have had a high score in life-change events one year, give yourself a break and keep things much the same as usual in the following twelve months, or at least attempt to avoid the high score changes. If that proves impossible, then make sure you have more rest than usual during the high score times to counteract the strain, and don't take on any unnecessary changes at that time. It is also important to ensure you are eating a good diet which supplies vital replenishment to your body's resources. In these ways you can help to strengthen the body's defences against illness and breakdown of health. (See Chapter 8 for advice on diet.)

Life Events Table

Events	Value
Death of a spouse	100
Divorce	73
Marital separation	65
Jail term	63
Death of close family member	63
Personal injury or illness	53
Marriage	50
Fired from work	47
Marital reconciliation	45
Retirement	45
Change in family member's health	44
Pregnancy	40
Sexual difficulties	39
Addition to family	39
Business readjustment	39
Change in financial status	38
Death of a close friend	37
Change to different type of work	36
Change in number of marital arguments	35
Mortgage or loan over £100,000	31
Foreclosure of mortgage or loan	30
Change in work responsibilities	29
Son or daughter leaving home	29
Trouble with in-laws	29
Outstanding personal achievement	28
Spouse begins or stops work	26
Starting or finishing school	26
Change in living conditions	25
Revision of personal habits	24
Trouble with boss	23
Change in work hours, conditions	20
Change in residence	20
Change in schools	20

Change in recreational habits	19
Change in church activities	19
Change in social activities	18
Mortgage or loan under £100,000	17
Change in sleeping habits	16
Change in number of family gatherings	15
Change in eating habits	15
Vacation	13
Christmas season	12
Minor violation of the law	11

Our cognitive interpretations of these life events also play a significant part. If something like a divorce is more of a relief than an agony it will not take such a toll on your health, although the actual changes involved will still have an impact on your adaptive energy. Some events will be experienced more traumatically by certain individuals than others, and will therefore be more depleting of the body's resources, a factor not taken sufficiently into account in the early research.

Your attitude can help

Each life event does not affect everyone in exactly the same way, and it has been discovered in more recent research that a person's attitudes can protect their body. I don't mean that you should artificially force yourself to experience joy in the face of sad events, but where it is possible and appropriate, altering one's attitude can do much to release stress, or at least to mitigate against its more extreme effects.

However serious your life circumstances, or however over-stretched you may feel, try to take regular time out for laughter, it is a real tonic. Laughing expels your breath and is followed by deep inhalation, which relaxes you. It distinctly elevates your mood, which has been found to raise the pain threshold as well as increasing the production of immunoglobulins, which help defend you against illness and infection. Laughter Clubs were started by a doctor in Mumbai, India, in 1995, where people gathered in the early morning for the sole purpose of laughing. Dr Madan Kataria recognised the physical and emotional health benefits that derive from regular laughter, and he developed a practice that combined yoga breathing, simple loosening exercises and laughing. There are now 8,000 Laughter Yoga Clubs in 65 countries worldwide. Dr Kataria's book, *Laugh for No Reason*, is available online. Find out more at www.laughteryoga.org (also see Useful Addresses for further information). I shall be saying much more regarding attitudinal approaches in many of the following chapters.

Dr Hans Selye was one of the pioneer researchers into the stress syndrome and its effects in the 1930s and 40s, and this is explained fully in his book, *The Stress of Life*, (McGraw-Hill, second revised edition, 1978). Dr Selye made an enormous contribution through his dedicated work, but I fear that his findings are not as well understood today as they might be. I shall attempt to translate the medical research into lay terms, as well as into practical, useful everyday applications for releasing your stress and feeling more in control of your life.

In relation to our limited adaptive capacity, Dr Selye wrote:

'It is as though, at birth, each individual inherited a certain amount of adaptation energy, the magnitude of which is determined by his genetic background, his parents. He can draw upon this capital thriftily for a long but monotonously uneventful existence, or he can spend it lavishly in the course of a stressful, intense, but perhaps more colourful and exciting life. In any case, there is just so much of it, and he must budget accordingly.'

Don't bankrupt your energy bank

If you don't budget, but overspend your adaptation energy by having to adapt or adjust to too many changes in too short a space of time, you become bankrupt in terms of energy, with nothing left over for an emergency, or for unexpected change. So pay vigilant attention to your energy bank, and try not to run it on permanent overdraft! Try to keep an ongoing energy 'savings account' so that you always have some reserves. In my opinion a great number of people nowadays are finding it a struggle to function well because they are in a state of permanent exhaustion due to the high levels of demand we all face each day. Therefore, it is not surprising that we feel strained and not terribly happy much of the time. You feel the most stress and lack of control when the demands of your life outstrip your resources. Many people spend their energy too freely and neglect to 'pay in' to their energy bank regularly; we need to build our energy levels and other resources constantly, and we shall be looking at how to do this in many different ways throughout this book.

Change is also stressful because it can feel threatening: it threatens what we know and all that is familiar and predictable. So, however inevitable change may be, it takes its toll – today more than ever before.

Mitigating the effects of change

Given that change is not going to go away, or slow down, and that in all probability it will increase and intensify, it is going to become ever more necessary that we take this phenomenon seriously and learn how to manage ourselves in relation to change.

So the first strategy in controlling stress must be to assess how much change you are currently coping with, or have been coping with in the recent past and whether or not you feel stressed by it.

Managing change means mitigating the effects of change: that is, to minimise them as much as possible and/or compensate yourself during the changes and afterwards. Some practical guidelines are outlined below:

- **Stagger different changes:** If you are faced with a number of inevitable or unavoidable changes, try at least to stagger them, with resting periods in-between each change so that you do not overload yourself with too much to adapt to in a short period of time.

- **Break up each change:** Every change can be broken into a number of stages, interspersed with time to rest and replenish yourself. If you cannot spread them out, but have to deal with many changes all at once, then plan some recovery time at the end of it all – time to do nothing very much while you adjust and acclimatise to the new situation or circumstances; time to recover your resources.

- **Take stock:** Most importantly, do not just lurch from adjustment to adjustment without taking stock of what is happening to you, because it will exhaust your capabilities and absolutely everything will then seem more difficult than usual, for you will be running on empty with no reserves.

- **Maintain equilibrium elsewhere:** If you know a large number of changes are coming up in one area of your life, make sure that you keep things much the same as usual in other areas. For example, supposing you have received promotion at work, have just moved to new offices, acquired a new boss and new work colleagues, and are possibly having to learn a completely new computer system or adjust to new working procedures, then it would be inadvisable to move house (a very stressful event), attempt to learn a foreign language and start flying lessons at the same time! In other words, don't take on any extra, unnecessary, demanding activities.

● **Take your time:** If, for example you have recently been divorced, been forced to move out of your home and perhaps had a reduction in income, then that is quite enough for anyone to cope with at any one time. Do not take on any more change until you have had time to become accustomed to the new circumstances. According to the Life Events Table, the most stressful change in anyone's life is the loss of an important relationship or bereavement. Such changes need a significant amount of time for adjustment to be made and should not be hurried or denied. You can probably understand how this kind of change in life circumstances depletes a person's resources, both emotionally and mentally, and how those stresses take their toll on the physical body. A person in this situation needs to be protected against any more stress, or change, and must give themselves permission not to take on too much until they feel stronger.

All loss has a major impact on our normal coping ability, and this applies equally to the loss of any part of our body, perhaps through surgery or accident, or the loss of usual use in certain limbs, as with paralysis, or disability like RSI (repetitive strain injury) or severe arthritis. All these things change your relationship with the world around you. Time is the greatest healer here and I would always advise: "Just take your own time to adjust; don't push yourself, or allow yourself to be pushed by others."

Coping with key stressful life events

A new baby

A mammoth change of lifestyle is experienced when a new baby is born, and often couples are not prepared for the toll this takes on their energies and adaptive capabilities. Many try to play down the change to their way of life, often because they don't feel ready to change anything, but in the first few months at least it is best to give yourselves plenty of 'floating' time with a minimum of demands in other areas. I think a great many new mothers become depressed due to exhaustion more than any other factor. They have high expectations of themselves, often expecting to be able to do everything they did before in addition to looking after their baby. But a baby's needs are many and unrelenting at first, and use up huge amounts of their mother's energy. Time is needed for adjustment to the new situation, not forgetting the internal changes and adjustments taking place in the new mother's hormone levels. Mothers must look after themselves as well as their newborn.

Starting school

Children starting school for the first time face enormous adjustments, which will be taxing to their adaptation energy and need to be taken into consideration when planning the rest of their timetable. The change of leaving the safe and relatively peaceful environment of home, to be confronted with scores of other children, new surroundings, new adults to relate to, on top of the strain of starting structured learning programmes, is all incredibly demanding and often not sufficiently understood by parents. It is little wonder that these children can be crabby and bad-tempered when they come out of school! I always found one of the best ways to counteract the irritability was to make sure I met my daughter with something to eat so as to raise her blood sugar level, a sticky bun or a sandwich or even some biscuits, which would supply instant sugar and cheer her up until she got home and could eat some better quality food. We are all irritable when our blood sugar is low.

Try to be patient with children starting school if they are difficult. They are just overloaded and need to get home to a protected, safe and quiet space where they can coast for a while. Equally, make sure that your child is not overloaded with extra changes outside school time, like ballet or music lessons, until they have adjusted. If possible, avoid dragging them around the supermarket after school, for that kind of environment provides too much sensory stimulation for a tired child, usually causing them to go into a hyperactive state, which frays everybody's nerves and often ends in arguments and tears. Protect and cosset them a little more than usual, and make sure they get sufficient sleep. Make bedtime calm, with stories, songs or nursery rhymes, after a warm, soothing bath.

Children often contract frequent minor illnesses when they start school, which is due in part to mixing with a large number of other children, but is also due to the increased demand on their adaptive energy leaving less energy available for the body to combat invading organisms. This phenomenon is also seen in adults undergoing demanding or stressful changes. Teachers starting a new school year usually go through a phase of increased susceptibility to illness, and the same has also been noticed among medical students during the first months of their training, as well as others in new and demanding situations.

Leaving for university

Another life change frequently experienced, but often underestimated, is leaving school and going to university. Suddenly, as an undergraduate, you have to cope with completely organising your timetable alone: shopping for food and feeding yourself adequately on a small budget, making sure you have clean clothes and clean surroundings. You are responsible for lots of tasks that were probably taken care of by someone else before – usually your mother – on top of the extra intellectual workload and this is not to mention the adjustment to new tutors and new housemates or fellow students in halls. There is a huge change in circumstances usually not sufficiently acknowledged or prepared for. No wonder many undergraduates become depressed. Actually, they are probably not truly clinically depressed, they are most likely to be buckling under too much demand for change all at once; it is exhausting their resources.

 Case study 1: The effects of change

A client of mine has recently split up with her long-term boyfriend, and because she was living with him in his apartment, she has had to move out. She is currently dividing her time between staying with two different friends who have offered to help, but who live on opposite sides of London, so she is spread between two homes with some of her things in each place. This is all very taxing to her emotional energy. She has lost her emotional partner and her home all at the same time and has no secure base from which to operate. She also has no territory to call her own and it is affecting her performance at work. She has had a number of negative confrontations with her boss for forgetting important tasks and she has begun to talk about changing her job. I am trying to dissuade her from this, for she will destabilise herself even further. She does not recognise the stress she is under and simply wants to get away from what she perceives as 'hassle', but another major change in an important area of her life will weaken her at this point – it will not improve matters. As much as possible, she needs to keep her life the same as usual while she adjusts to her new status. In a few months' time, when she has found a permanent home, she could start the search for a new job, but right now it would just add to the stress and strain to take on more change. I can only hope she will listen to my advice, but this is a good illustration of how intense life events can affect our capacity to cope in other areas.

We do adjust and adapt to changes given time. The new circumstances become the 'norm' and we acclimatise or habituate as psychologists like to say. In other words, the new has metamorphosed into the habitual, demanding less attention and therefore requiring less energy.

Some changes we choose and some are forced upon us. Try to assess how much change you are dealing with when you are feeling particularly stressed and strained and you may be surprised to realise how much change is, or has been, happening in your life. Also try to be aware of the changes that members of your family may be coping with, or in other close relationships (especially if you are experiencing difficulties with them) if people are more short-tempered than usual, or things blow up for no apparent reason. This could all be due to exhausted reserves of adaptation.

Keep reminding yourself that too much change in too short a space of time will be severely debilitating and may diminish your abilities in all areas of your life.

If most of the things you face each day feel more and more of a strain, even things that previously seemed relatively easy to cope with, this may indicate that you are handling too much change and exhausting your adaptation energy. So take mitigating, or compensating action as suggested above and throughout this book. In order to evade anymore demands on your overstretched resources you may even have to tell a 'white lie' or two. This is simply good life management and good sense!

Chapter 2

Wisdom and truth: vital resources

Hold on to what is valuable to you

It is not only the volume and speed of change that is stressing us. Many people feel uneasy about the *kind* of changes that are happening and our lack of control over them; this causes anxiety and emotional stress. For while a large number of today's changes may be exciting, interesting and 'good', a worrying level of what we are implementing is not good for us at all. Thus we are not only coping with rapid change, which can be overwhelming to our adaptation energy, but we also have to cope with the anxiety produced by all the 'wrong' things that are happening – the changes we perceive as bad for us, and for the planet. This is another load to carry. I am talking about things like cloning, polluted air, toxic waterways, gridlocked motorways, nuclear power plants and the transportation of nuclear waste, the devastation of the rainforests, climate change and much, much more that I shall come to later.

Is there anything we can do? Yes, I think there is, and I think it will have an influence eventually, firstly for our personal lives and then gradually for the whole planet.

I believe that the next most important step in our strategy to minimise and compensate for the strain and intensity of our changing world is to ensure that we consciously retain, and regularly focus on, all the wisdom that has been accumulated through the ages. Those wise directives that have been passed down through the generations – either verbally or by the written word – that instruct us in the best ways of living and behaving and which are in danger of being squeezed off the current agenda as we become increasingly seduced by the novelties of our techno-logical age. One very relevant saying I heard a while ago is:

'Where is the wisdom we have lost in knowledge, and where is the knowledge we have lost in information?'

It is tremendously important, in my view, both at a personal level and for humanity as a whole, that we don't lose sight of those eternal truths that do not change with changing fashions or new ideas – that do not go out of date – and which can give us a sense of stability, certainty and continuity in the face of change. These profound truths and wisdom have supported, sustained and in-spired humankind through many changing scenarios. We must not forget what we know. If we lose our connection to the wisdom of ages past and to fundamental, eternal truths, we shall have nothing to anchor us or sustain us in the face of life's challenges, and we'll go further and further astray.

In many ways you could say that all the answers we need are already with us, we just have to remind ourselves, search them out and apply them appropriately. This is one of the themes I shall be returning to again and again throughout the book. I shall search out the ancient wisdom teachings about different aspects of life and present them to you with suggestions about how to apply them in current living in order to control your stress levels. But I would also encourage you to work on doing the same: to discover, or remember, the wisdom or truths that make sense to you, and give regular time to reflect on them.

They may come from a spiritual or religious belief system, a philosophical viewpoint or the wise traditions that have been passed down through the ages in each culture. They are the cornerstones of civilised life, and can act as touchstones when we feel overwhelmed or bewildered by all the demands of today's changing world that clamour for our attention. We need these guiding principles for our total well-being, and if we return to these messages of truth and wisdom regularly throughout our day, we will know how to respond, what is best practice or the right basis for our approach to almost everything. They provide a calming point of certainty within the rapidly shifting, superficial values of our contemporary culture.

Allow yourself moments of stillness

Don't just rush through your day, but be still from time to time and call to mind the fundamental truths you know. Give yourself a few minutes, three or four times a day, to stop whatever you are doing and to step back, mentally, to focus on something that has a deeper meaning for you than your daily concerns; something that resonates for you as an eternal truth.

The test of a truth is that it can be applied at any time, in any situation, and so can transcend opinion or prejudice, and can speak to each and every human being regardless of race or creed. A truth always resonates as being true, so it provides an extra dimension. It expands the viewpoint in any situation and it endures across the years.

⋏ Exercise: Determine your core values

What is your bottom line? What are your core values? Which are your own truths and guiding principles?

Write a list of all the most important truths that you use to support you in living your life, or those that you would like to implement more often. It may take you a while to bring these things up into your consciousness, but if you give it the time and the serious consideration it deserves, you will find this mental exercise enormously rewarding and uplifting.

Carry your list of truths around with you, to refer to when you feel blown off course – when you feel anxious, not at peace, stressed – to reassure you, and to remind you where the firm ground lies. Pin up copies of your list somewhere in your home and work-place, even in your car (perhaps especially in your car!) so that you are constantly in touch with these foundation stones of life.

Love changes everything

I don't think anyone would deny the power of love. This truth has been recognised and expressed in different ways throughout all recorded ages. One beautiful example is the twentieth-century song by Andrew Lloyd Webber which asserts that 'Love changes everything.' **Love Changes Everything. This is a true statement.**

✗ Exercise: Change the perspective

Write 'love changes everything' on a beautiful piece of paper, carry it around with you, and look at it often. Call this to mind whenever you are in a difficult situation or are having problems with someone, and see if it changes the way you look at things.

On the theme of love, it is useful to remember the words of the thirteenth-century physician Paracelsus, who is reported to have said:

'Love is the highest level of medicine.'

This is an extraordinary statement that certainly deserves thinking about. It indicates the enormous power of love – the power to heal. I believe this is an important truth.

In the Bible, Christ is reported to have said:

'Love one another.'

Buddha said:

'Let a man overcome anger by love.'

Buddha also stated:

'Hatred is never conquered by hatred at any time; hatred is conquered by love.'

I am sure each of you reading this will have your own favourite sayings about the power of love. It may be a line from a poem or a quote from Shakespeare, such as these lines from Sonnet 116:

'Love is not love
Which alters when it alteration finds,
Or bends with the remover to remove:
O no! it is an ever-fixed mark
That looks on tempests and is never shaken;'

Of course, it is not easy to love everyone, but just start by trying to like people a bit more; look for the things that are likeable in another person, there is always something to find if you try.

Plato's words are helpful here:

'Be kind, for everyone you meet is fighting a harder battle.'

We are often afraid of other people and assume they will criticise us, but there is actually no reason not to love, for we don't know what is taking place in someone else's mind. Why do we feel frightened of them? Why not decide they are lovable? It all starts with us, after all; we are responsible for the attitudes with which we approach the outer world and each other. When we choose to love, it really does change everything.

So whenever you are experiencing difficulties with someone, make the decision to love them. Try to *feel* love for them. See them not as a giant enemy, but as a fallible and flawed human being trying their best to cope, loaded down as we all are with their problems and worries. Deciding to love them will change the way you deal with them.

In *The Little Book of Wisdom* (published by Rider), His Holiness the Dalai Lama says:

> *'Practice love. To do so in all situations will take time, but you should not lose courage. If we wish happiness for mankind, love is the only way.'*

Another way of applying this truth is to make a decision to try to understand. Trying to understand another will always change the way you relate to them. Try to put yourself in their shoes. When we truly understand we develop compassion, and compassion produces love.

In *The Little Book of Wisdom*, the Dalai Lama also says:

> *'Inner tranquillity comes from the development of love and compassion.'*

The theologian and philosopher Albert Schweitzer once stated:

> *'Until he extends his circle of compassion to all living things, man will not find peace.'*

This is an example of how an eternal truth can help you to find the solution or way through something difficult or stressful. It changes the perspective. It expands your viewpoint, enabling you to look at the situation or relationship from a new level – the level of eternal, unchanging truth. This level will always help you to find answers, or clues, for coping with life and controlling your stress. It removes you away from the level of stress.

It is important to find your own eternal truths and pieces of recorded wisdom and say them to yourself regularly in your mind and in your heart, referring to your written list to remind you. Find and affirm what has meaning for you, and then find ways to apply these truths in your life by letting them influence your behaviour. Repeat these truths and words of wisdom to yourself many times a day, especially if you feel wound up, stressed or upset. Words have a great power to influence our inner state.

The power of the right word

Saying the right words, whether internally or out aloud, can have a profound effect on how you think and how you feel, strengthening you inwardly. The more you repeat positive words and phrases the more they will have a positive influence on you.

Repetition enhances the neural pathways in the brain for a particular thought. We must not forget that our thoughts are real. They produce electromagnetic and chemical signals across different networks of our brain cells. Also remember, it is only you who can talk to you inside your mind! We need these inner affirmations to help us through the many difficulties of today's world where there is so much sadness, violence and ignorance. We need constant reminders of the positive, beautiful and true. They are the counterbalance. Just try this frequently for a few days and see how much better you feel, how released you feel.

⅄ Exercise: Harnessing the power of repetition

Try repeating just one relevant word at regular moments throughout the day, such as: peace, serenity, calm, tranquillity, joy or love.
Alternatively, find your own special word. I often put two together;
I frequently say to myself 'peace and love'. This may sound like a
hippy greeting but I find it very calming. It reminds me of what's
really important and it particularly helps me if I'm dealing with
someone who is making me irritated or angry.

One helpful phrase I often use to myself is: **'Rise above it!'** My
very wise father used to say that to me when I was young and
would get into a state about someone or something that upset me.
It's a great statement and works on many levels. It can remind me
not to be petty or small-minded. It reminds me that I can conquer
my negative emotions, that I am not a victim and that I have a
choice about how to behave. It reminds me to act from my bigger
self, not my little self. It feels comforting. I fill my mind with the
words, and mentally take off to the higher ground.

You might like to use my phrase, or you may find others that help
you, such as:

- Do unto others as you would they do unto you.
- Silence is golden.
- To every thing there is a season, and a time to every purpose
  under heaven.
- Judge not, lest you yourself be judged.
- Life is meaningful when our hearts are full of love.

Use whatever feels appropriate for you. Use the ancient wisdoms
as they were intended to be used as a kind of life support system
or a blueprint from which everything ripples out. They change

your inner state and as a result you have a different influence on those around you. This is how truth ripples out into the world, the planet and the universe.

You may not always be able to rise to the level of truth, but just knowing there is another way to see things, another way to behave, can help you control your stress levels. Many research studies have shown that a strong spiritual, religious or philosophical belief system is an important factor in maintaining good mental and physical health, and buffers one against stress, especially the stress of change or loss.

Writing down meaningful statements makes them feel more real, it makes them physically manifest. Also, when you look at them you imprint them in your mind; you *remind* yourself of their reality and truth. As I said above, they act as a counterbalance to the many dark and troubling images regularly presented to our minds through the media. I think we have to work at providing positive and uplifting thoughts and images for ourselves, to nourish and soothe our minds. Carry them around with you in your pocket or bag and take them out to read from time to time, or simply touch the paper on which they are written and imagine the wise words being absorbed by your fingers, travelling up your arms and into your heart and mind. Feel reassured just knowing what they tell you: let them strengthen you.

If you were not brought up in any belief system, or cannot connect with any customs or traditions, look at the positive side of this. It leaves you free to find your own belief structure, to mix different cultural thoughts or different spiritual beliefs in a way that makes sense to you. You are not constrained by just one belief system that dictates it is the 'right' one. I personally believe that all truth comes from the same source. I think all the religions in the world are talking about the same thing in different ways.

There are many paths to the top of the mountain, but there is only one mountain top. So truth is truth in every language and in every different way it may be expressed.

There are so many books around nowadays containing gems of wisdom and spiritual guidance from numerous sources. If you need inspiration visit your local bookstore and browse among the treasures and riches that have been put into print. Some are little pocket books, available at low cost, one or two of which you might find supportive to carry around with you. They will transport you to that other dimension we have been considering when you feel bogged down, overwhelmed, disillusioned or stressed. (See Further Reading.)

Your personal truth

Equally important, of course, are our own personal truths. Whatever is valuable to you and sustains you in a personal way must not be neglected or lost along the way in the rush of daily living. It is important to honour consciously whatever you have recognised as a fundamental truth in your own experience of life, or simply whatever is significant in your own way of living your life. It could be the social customs or manners you were taught as a child, the 'rules' or guiding principles that were operating in your family, or possibly a particular member of your family or a teacher at school who inspired you with an inner desire to imitate their standards or achievements. As children we so often recognise the truths which transcend everyday concerns. As adults we must not lose the connection. We must remember what we have always known. I think our truths need to be polished up and put on display in our lives – like valuable possessions in a wealthy household. We must be proud of displaying our spiritual wealth. It is, after all, our valuable legacy from the past.

In addition, remember things which comforted or uplifted you when you were young, like special stories or poems, or particular toys that had a significant meaning for you, perhaps because they symbolised some positive quality like kindness, playfulness or joy and happiness. Do not neglect them – hold on to whatever is of value to you. These are our personal comforters, which can encourage and reassure us when the going gets rough, and must be kept in place, in our inner world, alongside the innovative and new, in order that the right balance is maintained. It is important to keep the continuum, the connection to our personal and ancestral roots.

As I have indicated above, I believe that many of the answers to today's stress-inducing problems, and to questions about how to structure our lives, are to be found in the ancient wise teachings of all of the different cultures: they can form a sort of bottom line, or the strong foundations upon which we can build and rebuild continuously. I feel they have even greater relevance for today than ever before as they often restore a sense of calm and serenity that counterbalances the strain and rush.

It is important that we do not just race headlong into the future at great speed without a backward glance, throwing the baby out with the bath water and forgetting, neglecting or rejecting all that has been learnt by previous generations and other cultures – all the customs, traditions and beliefs that the wise elders recognised as essential to happiness and well-being. Many of today's problems exist because we are failing to include these fundamental cornerstones in much of modern life; we have destabilised ourselves. In the *Bhagavad-Gita* it is written:

'The wise say, My Lord! That they are forever lost, whose ancient traditions are lost.'

We must find ways to apply wisdom teachings from the past to the modern context. This must form part of our strategy otherwise we are left with insufficient familiar ground under our feet. It may be exciting to embrace and consume all that is new, but we are getting horribly out of balance.

Equally undesirable obviously, is that we overreact in the opposite direction by hanging on to the old ways no matter what, resisting and blocking everything new that threatens to separate us from our comfortable preconceived ideas and habits. We should not feel threatened by the new, but equally we should not feel obliged to give up too readily all that has supported us previously. We need to give ourselves permission and the confidence to hold on to certain things and certain ways of doing things if they are right for us, in any of the areas of our lives, at the same time as opening ourselves to embrace the new age in which we live.

Recipes for life

Life is a little like cooking a favourite recipe. For it to be successful you have gradually learnt what extra ingredients to include, what ingredients to cut down on and what to leave out altogether because that's what suits your taste and the taste of your family or friends. But if you leave out certain vital ingredients then the result will be disappointing, and if you hand on that incomplete recipe to future generations they would never know the true taste of the particular dish unless someone remembers what had been forgotten and rewrites the recipe.

A recipe for living

Mix 3 kilos of patience with 2 kilos of tolerance: leave to mature. Then add 3 large cups of loving kindness and 2 dessertspoons of sweetness. Leave to stand for an hour or two. Blend in a large cupful of humour, a pinch of cynicism and 1 tablespoon of judgement. After 2 days, taste for reality. Add 1 teaspoon of anger, 2 cups of creativity, 3 cups of flexibility and 1 tablespoon of open-mindedness. Shake, don't stir.

I do think we are currently in the process of creating a somewhat poisonous recipe for life; one that is definitely under-nourishing, and which leaves out many essential ingredients. This must not be handed down to future generations: we must rethink what we are putting into the pot of daily life. What are we telling our children? Do we want to hand on recipes that are under-nourishing?

𝘟 Exercise: Serving up your own recipe for life

Take time to write the recipe for your life remembering not to leave out all that is true and valuable to you. Have fun with this and enjoy connecting to your creativity. Allow yourself space and quality time for reflection, it will give you a sense of serenity and peace. Then pin this recipe up in your kitchen, and every time you enter that room you will be reminded not to leave out the most important ingredients for a nourishing and sustaining lifestyle. If this feels too difficult then just list your own personal truths, to carry with you as a calming, de-stressing, inspirational checklist. Best of all, do both!

You could get really creative and write out a recipe for each of the most important aspects of your life. For example: a recipe for raising children, a recipe for a wonderful holiday, a recipe for family life, a recipe for a productive work team, a recipe for a successful company, a recipe for a happy old age and so on. By working on this you cast a brighter light on what is important for you and you see yourself more clearly.

Inspirational wisdom and eternal truths

Below is a list of truths and wise teachings or sayings that I find inspiring and which give me guiding principles for living my life. You may like to use this as a starting point for creating one of your own. Add to it on an ongoing basis as you discover a truth which inspires, comforts or calms you, or when you remember some wise quotation from a book, a poem or a song, your Bible or any other spiritual teaching – or your mother.

My Personal List of Inspirational Wisdom and Eternal Truths

Always respond intelligently, even to unintelligent treatment – *Chuang-Tzu*

Do no harm – *Buddhist teaching*

He that findeth wisdom, findeth life – *Book of Proverbs*

The first duty of love is to listen – *Paul Tillich, theologian and philosopher*

To understand is to forgive – *my own saying*

All we have to do is become who we have always been – *Carl Gustav Jung*

This above all, to thine own self be true – *William Shakespeare*

Look after your body as if you will live for a thousand years, and your soul as if you will die tomorrow – *Sufi teaching*

Noblesse oblige – this means: with privilege comes responsibility

There's a lot of good in the worst of us
And a lot of bad in the best of us
So it ill behoves the most of us

To talk about the rest of us
– *I love this little rhyme, quoted to me as a child*

Live and let live – *an important injunction for tolerance, for letting others be*

In peace there is an end to all misery – *The Bhagavad-Gita*

It is better to light one small candle than to bemoan the darkness – *Carl Gustav Jung*

If at first you don't succeed, try, try, try again – *old wives' saying*

Never let the sun go down on your wrath – *from the Bible*: meaning we should try to resolve conflicts with others, or within ourselves, as soon as possible rather than carrying resentment and anger around with us for days, months or even years

There is only one success: to be able to spend your life in your own way – *Christopher Morley*

As you sow, so shall you reap – *Jesus of Nazareth*

The fruit of love is service, which is compassion in action – *Mother Teresa*

All you need is love – *The Beatles (one of the wisest sayings – ever!)*

... and all the other quotes throughout this book

Do it your way

In more mundane terms, the principle of not giving up on things from the past that comfort you also applies. If some aspect of technology frustrates or confounds you, don't bother with it. Use what you like and leave what you can't, or don't want, to handle. For example, if you prefer to continue to use the telephone rather than send emails, then assert your right, to yourself, to communicate in this way as much as you choose, in the way that suits you and your individual temperament.

I read a lovely piece in a recent publication which was reported to have come originally from the actor and comedian Rowan Atkinson; he allegedly said that if email had preceded the invention of the telephone, everyone would have hailed the arrival of the phone as the greatest technological breakthrough of recent times. He apparently added, 'Consider this: no longer do you have to type words into the ether hoping that someone will type back. You actually speak to someone on a gizmo that lets you and the recipient of your *bons mots* hear and talk to each other in real time!' This is exactly the kind of thinking that is needed to control our stresses, it is lateral thinking par excellence or in other words, thinking for oneself rather than following the general consensus. Do it your way!

In another interview a well-known author revealed that she does not use a computer or word processor, as might be expected, or even a typewriter, but that she writes her books and film scripts in pencil with a good old-fashioned rubber eraser nearby. That's her way. We each have to find 'our own way': the way that is right for us. If the old ways work for you, think very carefully before abandoning them. Believe in yourself and in your own, unique, individual way.

Things do not necessarily have more value just because they are new. Some of the old tools, or old attitudes may be more useful or efficient, or life-enhancing, than those that came after them. But make up your own mind. Don't allow yourself to be coerced into having to adopt every new gadget and technology that comes along just because it's there, hence loading yourself up with more to adjust to and learn, and increasing the amounts of information for your tired brain to absorb, leading to ever more stress and strain and less and less time for other aspects of life. For example, do you really have to respond to every telephone call, text message or email the moment it arrives?

Be in the here and now

Not so long ago if you were out walking in a park, or if you were enjoying dining out with a friend, the telephone was at home and could not interrupt your immediate experience or load you up with more to think about than was in your present moment. Nowadays, it's considered normal for most people to spend a huge percentage of every day engaged with their mobile technology, their smartphone, iPad, tablet or whatever new invention has just appeared. But this has inherent dangers in that we are disengaging with the people and things that are around us in real time. Being focused on mobile technology takes people's awareness away from their immediate environment, which means they don't notice what is around them and they may even miss some exquisite moments which could be uplifting. They may not notice a beautiful cloud formation in the sky, a sunset, or the blossom on a tree in spring, a child's laughter or just other people walking by, attractive shop windows or posters advertising interesting events.

Control your use of technology

Don't allow technology to control you! Technology is taking us away from the 'here and now', which means we are not living sufficiently in the present moment. I think this is quite serious. People are becoming more focused on screens than on actual life. We are growing blind to what is happening around us with the result that we are becoming increasingly insensitive to the people we encounter in our daily living. We've all experienced the effects of this lack of awareness, such as bumping into people in the street without apologising or not engaging in human interaction at the checkout counter. Technology has a place, but don't allow it to obscure your view of the 'here and now', especially when you are in the company of others. I think it is very sad, for example, to see couples in a restaurant texting or talking on their mobile phones to people who are not present rather than talking to each other. We should be concerned that we are behaving increasingly more like robots than human beings.

Don't allow technology to intimidate or overwhelm you. Keep reminding yourself that it is all there to act as your slave, not the other way round! Technology is speeding up our lives, making us busier than ever. We are all struggling to keep up with the input from emails, texts and social media networks, so that rather than simplifying life and giving us greater freedom, technology does seem to be enslaving us. We have to guard against becoming too dependent on it all. We are getting to the point where we can't function without it – a rather dangerous place to be, in my opinion. When your machines break down, or fail to function, don't automatically assume that it is somehow you who are inadequate. Machines do break down, it is all part of the stress of life, and the only thing you can do is not overload yourself with guilt or anger about it; accept it and be patient, especially with yourself. (See Chapter 4 for more on technology and stress.)

Today's world requires constant discrimination, and we are going to have to exercise it very powerfully in order not to lose control of our lives, our joy and our dreaming/creative time. We have to find a stance that is open to the new, but not destabilised by being empty because we have thrown out all the old valuables.

'And/and' not 'either/or'

In psychology there is an idea that could be applied usefully here: it is the notion of 'and/and' rather than 'either/or'. What this means is that instead of putting things in opposition to each other and then having to decide which is better, or more desirable than the other – possibly causing yourself much inner turmoil and conflict – you adopt an inclusive stance of embracing them both at the same time. In other words, of seeing that the merits of one do not negate the merits of the other; that each has a place. One may be right at one time, or in a certain situation, and the other at another time or in other circumstances. Or both may be 'best' in different ways. This really is very freeing.

Whenever you find yourself in a dilemma of duality with the question: 'Is it this, or is it that?' try answering yourself with: 'It's both,' and see if this makes the situation both easier and clearer. Or if you are asking yourself: 'Should I do this or that?' answer: 'Both', and see what a difference it makes to the tension and stress. I don't mean that you should load yourself up with more and more things to do, but that you ease the inner stress by seeing how two seemingly opposing things can both be the right way to proceed. Maybe you can even mix them together with a little from one and something from the other to arrive at a more creative outcome. The more you are able to grasp and adopt this 'and/and' principle in your life, the more you will find a way through potential conflicts.

There is no *one* right way of doing things, but many right ways. We need a variety of ideas and insights and we need the flexibility to embrace many possibilities. Flexibility is going to be one of the most important attributes to foster in the coming years.

Find the 'Third Point'

In every dilemma there is always a third point: a position that stands a little apart from any extremes that are in opposition to each other, and from where you can assess dispassionately what is valuable about both. Finding the third point enables you to lift yourself out of the tension in a situation and to look at it more objectively. It's the 'Rise above it' injunction that my father used to deliver to me whenever I got upset about someone or something.

Think of yourself standing at the apex of a triangle, above the duality, and from here you are able to see that everything is part of the whole. In other words, that everything has a place. It is enormously releasing. A practical example is this: imagine you are in an argument with your partner, or a friend, that is getting you nowhere; the third point would be to introduce something outside the argument. It might be looking out of a window and saying 'Just look at that beautiful sky', so that you take the other person's attention to another place – it can be called distraction – but it frees the situation by introducing something new. This is especially useful if you're dealing with a child having a temper tantrum. Don't react to what the child is doing as that simply reinforces it. Instead, distract the child's attention away from the immediate problem. You introduce something new, and so the previous situation is immediately changed. In any conflict situation, always try to find the third point, something outside the problem, and experience for yourself how it changes the perspective.

We need to find a balanced path between the old ideas and practices and new innovations, valuing what is good in each. I believe it is our challenge at the present moment in history to get the mix right between the past that is worth retaining, the wisdom of past generations, and the new ideas that are born from a future vision. It is important in any situation that you attempt to hold this balance, retaining what is good while welcoming what is new, rather than allowing one automatically to negate the other.

✗ Exercise: Maintaining the equilibrium within

- Whenever you are in a state of crisis, stress or confusion put your physical body into an upright posture.
- Stand with your feet slightly apart, firmly planted on the ground, with your arms outstretched at either side, away from your body; imagine your right arm is reaching into the unknown future, and your left arm is connecting you to the past.
- Experience the stability of your legs and feet firmly placed on the ground and feel your body perfectly balanced in the present moment, between the past and the future.
- Now confirm to yourself that you are anchored securely in all that you know to be true and right from past experience, then feel the certainty of all you know moving in a vertical line through your body, starting from your head down to your heart, and then through your body down to your feet; now up through your heart to your head and mind again. This experience goes all through you and is not just in your head.
- Whatever is pulling at you on either side, whether from the past or the future, will not have the power to destabilise you. You affirm a core of certainty running through your whole being, like a seam of silver running through a rock.

This is a centring and stabilising exercise. Repeat it as many times as necessary, and then open yourself up to whatever you need to face and to deal with.

Do not be destabilised by forgetting to hold onto what you already know. We are often thrown into the panic of feeling ourselves in a vacuum of nothingness when we are stressed or anxious. Support yourself by affirming all that you know to be true. Then from that stable position you can be receptive to whatever else is demanding your attention.

This chapter is aimed at helping you to a state of greater equilibrium within yourself. Use these suggestions in your own way, but heed the message: do not throw the baby out with the bath water! Remember what your personal eternal truths are and hold onto what is valuable to you.

Chapter 3

Who is in control?

One of the truths that does not change however much the external circumstances change, is that as members of the species *Homo sapiens* we have very distinct and fundamental needs which have to be met if we are to feel relatively happy or contented, anxiety-free, comfortable and well. Not paying sufficient attention to any of these needs will make us more susceptible to stress.

We have already identified our need for some things to remain the same as a stabilising bedrock in a climate of change, also the need to retain the wisdom of the past and our connection to truth, as well as the need to stay within the limit of our adaptation energy. Another of our most important basic needs, however, is to feel in control of our lives and ourselves. Feeling out of control, or without sufficient control, is one of the major triggers to feeling stressed, and has been found to have negative implications for health.

Knowing that you have a satisfactory level of control over the world around you is good for your immune system and your heart. It has been demonstrated in experiments with animals that having no control over various stress factors suppressed immune function to a significant degree, while animals subjected to the same stresses but given some control over them did not suffer the same internal damage.

In one long-term study of a colony of monkeys, those creatures who had little or no control over the ordering of the hierarchy, and who were continually dominated by larger, more powerful monkeys, eventually developed high blood pressure followed by heart disease, due to the clogging up of their coronary arteries. This was despite eating the same diet, living in the same habitat and having the same degree of physical freedom as the higher status animals. In other words, the only difference was in their total lack of control over their environment and the behaviour displayed towards them by others in the society. The high status monkeys were found to have completely unclogged arteries. However, there was an unexpected discovery in this study. Some of the low-status monkeys managed to find a role for themselves by grooming their superiors and acting as helpers, with some of the low-status males playing with the young baby monkeys (it is normally unheard of for young males to take any interest in babies). By acting in this way they developed less severe atherosclerosis (hardening of the arteries) than those monkeys who were cowed by, and acquiesced to, their powerlessness. This seemed to point to the fact that if you can exercise a degree of autonomy, even in oppressive conditions, there will be less damage to your health.

A similar study involving civil servants, called the Whitehall Study, was carried out by London University over a period of 30 years. To their surprise, the lowest occurrence of heart disease was found among the highest level employees whom they had thought would be suffering from so-called 'executive stress'. However, those people at the top of the hierarchy had a high degree of control, which seemed to induce good health. Heart disease rates got worse as you went down the grades. It was discovered that early death rates were three times higher among junior office workers than among the senior civil servants. Only 40% of this difference could be explained by lifestyle factors (diet, exercise and smoking). It was concluded that the longer life expectancy in the more senior ranks was 60% due to having a high level of control and high status in the hierarchy. Similar conclusions have been drawn from other studies. High status, of course, implies control and autonomy: the freedom to make your own decisions and not feel oppressed, controlled or blocked by others.

A disturbing paradox of modern life, however, is that while we have increasing numbers of gadgets and technologies supposedly designed to give us freedom and independence, at the same time we are discovering that we actually have less and less control over numerous aspects of our lives. I believe we need to address this very consciously. The more aware we make ourselves of our stress factors, the more we can alter our behaviours and internal responses, both physiologically and attitudinally, so that they do not damage our health.

A great deal of the stress experienced today, and its outward expression of anger, is connected with the expectation that we should be able to control things, but in fact we can't! We own motor cars – once seen as ultimate symbols of independence and freedom – but we cannot drive them comfortably because too many other people also own cars and slow us down to a snail's pace or get in our way! We have developed wondrous modes of communication, but it is increasingly frustrating trying to get hold of a human being at the end of a telephone line without having to listen to endless recorded instructions about pressing buttons and wasting huge amounts of time. Emails are great except that we're now swamped with receiving too many, especially the ones from people trying to sell us things we don't want! This is not to mention the emails that disappear into the ether and are never answered.

In a sense we have set ourselves up. We have come to rely more and more on machines, gadgets and gizmos, which, when they don't work as they are supposed to, put us into a state of impotence. In addition, many of the structures and organisations that direct and control the various facets of modern living, or which are supposed to serve us, have become so huge and centralised, bogged down in bureaucracy and procedures, that they can make us feel threatened or powerless and overwhelmed by the difficulty of trying to interact with them. We certainly do not often feel that we can control them, or even the way they treat us.

We are confronted daily by frustration due to this increasing lack of control which, if it has no outlet or is not handled in the right way, can lead to a range of health problems including: high blood pressure, digestive disorders, irritable bowel syndrome, duodenal ulcers, disordered breathing patterns or panic attacks: these are all manifestations of inner tensions.

It is extremely important that we learn some strategies for handling the internal anger that is, quite understandably, triggered by the stress of not being able to have the level of control we would like. Internal anger as a result of feeling disempowered also often leads to depression. This is due to the energy being used to suppress the anger, which results in less being available for enjoyable living. Anger, of course, is suppressed because we know there is no point in getting angry with large corporations or machines. There is a very apt saying:

Impression without expression leads to depression.

In this chapter we are going to look at ways of altering our attitudinal approach, so as not to damage our health. Later in the book, in Chapters 8 and 9, you will find ways of addressing the physical aspects of stress, anger and anxiety, and combating the potentially damaging physiological changes that take place within our bodies when we become stressed and frustrated or feel threatened in some way. It is vital to learn how to take more control of these responses so that you can choose to react in the way that is best for your health and well-being, both mentally and physically.

Strategy No 1: Acceptance

When you absolutely cannot control a situation, the best and healthiest way of coping is to practise **acceptance**. If there is nothing you can do about it, let it go. Don't get wound up and angry because you will simply jeopardise your health without solving the problem.

Recognising when there is nothing you can do is wisdom. There is no point resisting something that you cannot change, like a traffic jam, a delayed plane or train or a machine that refuses to respond: it just winds you up and wastes your energy. Acceptance is not resignation; it is the recognition of reality, not denying that something is as it is. In fact, paradoxically, once you practice acceptance you will often begin to find ways around the situation, or whatever is facing you, because you are no longer putting all your energy and focus into the resistance and denial. Acceptance relaxes you. When you are relaxed you are more in harmony with yourself, and can connect more freely with your creativity and innovation.

I am reminded of the serenity prayer which was so popular a few years ago. It may seem a little clichéd now, but the message is sound. Let me remind you:

*'Lord, grant me the **Serenity** to accept the things I cannot change;*
*The **Courage** to change the things I can;*
*And the **Wisdom** to know the difference.'*

It might strike a chord with some of you, and the thoughts are sensible stress control. You might like to write it down and carry it around with you or pin it up in your home or workspace, or wherever you feel the most frustration in your life, perhaps your car! Or keep it in your pocket to read when faced with yet another delayed train.

Strategy No 2: Walk away

If you feel unable to control a situation sufficiently and you cannot accept it or find a way round it, another healthy reaction would be to decide to turn your back on it. That way you have regained control and decided on the action you will take. This is empowering. Walking away or cutting off from something may be the wisest choice you can make at that time.

It's all too big

John Betjeman, our late Poet Laureate, who was also a knowledgeable commentator on architecture, once said to me:

'The trouble with skyscrapers is that they bear no relationship whatsoever to the proportions of the human body, and therefore we cannot relate to them with any sense of comfort.'

Isn't this true of so much of today's world? It is out of proportion in relation to individual human beings, and many people when faced with these giant corporations and huge impersonal civic structures feel alienated, confused, diminished or uninvolved. I think this phenomenon can be seen in the reducing numbers of the electorate who turn out to vote, for example, or in the way we 'blank' each other in much of our daily activity, the supermarket queue, or at the bus stop. It is all so big that it is difficult to relate to and we can't control it! We feel disempowered and therefore we opt out. It is often easier to say to ourselves that we just don't care rather than to struggle with feeling ineffectual.

There certainly seems to be an increasing tendency to withdraw more and more into our own personal, smaller worlds and this is very sensible practice in certain circumstances. I would always advise that you withdraw for a while when you feel overwhelmed, because we cannot take on the whole world, the whole time. However, when carried to extremes, enclosing ourselves too exclusively in our own worlds can and does have negative consequences for local communities, as well as for us individually. The more we cut ourselves off from each other, the more we encourage misunderstanding. We are also in danger of missing out on what others could give to us if we were more open to receive their input. The answer is to take control in the right ways and not be pushed into reactionary measures or extreme positions.

Strategy No 3: Make a positive decision

Another way to feel more in control generally is in making decisions. When we make the right decisions we feel in control, not perhaps of the situation or circumstances, but of ourselves and our actions. Sometimes that is the only control we can have. If it is appropriate, deciding on a plan of action for making some changes that will give us more control is always energising, and beginning to implement the action is always empowering.

We can also make a decision to put ourselves into more situations where we *can* exercise control, to balance out the areas where we have little or no power. This could be in leisure-time activities like sport where we can control our own performance or in creative activities and hobbies, which give greater scope for controlling our timetables, expressing our individuality and the way we set about tasks.

Another positive decision would be to make sure we spend more time with people with whom we feel equal, and with the people who listen to us and respect our right to have an opinion or a 'say' about a situation or an outcome. This allows us to be more fully our true self, which is always empowering.

It is extremely important to remember that we always have the option of taking control of ourselves: of our actions and reactions as well as our inner attitudes.

The stress of capitalism and the consumer society

Of course, we can't opt out forever, or continually walk away, these are just strategies to control stress in the moment. Sooner or later we have to opt back in again and resume the struggle. It is often difficult to stand back and analyse very clearly what is happening when we live with something on a daily basis, but in the long-term we may have to adjust our thinking in order to cope with the environment in which we now find ourselves. Therefore, the more we can become aware of how we are 'set up' the more we can do to change the way we relate to it. Even if you can't change the outside world, you can change the way you interact with it, and this is the next strategy I want to put before you.

Most of us live in the capitalist or 'consumer' society, and the very nature of this society puts great pressure on all of us. The important point about the capitalist system is that it *needs* to control us if it is to function successfully; it must seduce us, or manipulate us, into maximum consumption. This is another important aspect of the stress of today's world that I believe we need to address consciously. We are under incessant commercial pressure, which causes subliminal stresses and anxieties due to the subtle coercion on our conscious control and the activating of our insecurities.

The consumer myth

To keep us engaged or to entice us back into the consumer relationship, large, impersonal organisations and civic authorities put out cosy, intimate advertisements to lull us into believing that they relate to us as individuals; that they care about us. We are cosseted and wooed as if we matter to them and are seduced by their illusion that fulfilment and happiness will be achieved with the acquisition of more things. In truth, these organisations only relate to us as figures on a balance sheet. Each individual is seen simply as a unit of ingestion, as a consumer of as much as possible, in order to maximise those profits. This explains the bad service, and extra frustration, you receive from those 'lovely people' in that television ad. The company and the advertisement are unconnected; it is all part of the manipulation, the mirage that is created to part you from your money. It is the consumer myth and you have no control over it. But worse, it is having a stressful influence on you. It undermines your self-esteem. For no matter how much we all realise that the unrealistic promises implied in many ads are pure fantasy creations, if you absorb an image on a regular basis it will eventually make a lasting impression.

When we continually see perfect-looking people with enviable lifestyles, it is bound to make us feel anxious about how well we are doing in our own lives. The consumer myth encourages unhappiness and envy as we compare ourselves with those beautiful beings in the advertisements, who have perfect hair, gleaming white teeth and fabulous bodies, and who are seen living in immaculately clean and stylish, luxurious homes with that expensive car in the driveway! It takes a strong person to stand apart from it all, someone with a very powerful sense of self. The pressure to be more physically perfect and have more possessions creates discontentment and erodes inner peace, causing much unconscious stress as well as tempting people to spend more than they can afford, leading to loss of financial control.

This may all seem obvious, but the important point is that we acknowledge consciously to ourselves just what is happening, why we feel these frustrations or impotency and where we feel them the most – in which parts of our daily lives. If we can indentify the sources of our stress triggers we can diminish their impact. When something is having an unconscious influence on you it is at its most powerful – you cannot deal with an unseen enemy or an unacknowledged one. It is a little like a food allergy: if you can identify which food is causing the undesirable symptoms you can eliminate it from your diet. If, however, you do not know what is causing your symptoms then you are a victim of them.

We are in a conundrum of conflict in today's world, empowered and disempowered at the same time. This lies at the heart of much of the stress we experience, and it applies to all of us, both in the developed and developing countries, for we have been given to expect much, at all levels of society, and yet delivery is somehow always happening tomorrow. Contentment eludes us. But, of course, we are looking for contentment in the wrong place, and I shall expand on this later.

When we see things for what they are we can deal with them more effectively and then have the possibility of taking control. If we are in control, we will understand the consumer trick; we will of course purchase the things we need but we will not get hung up on consuming for any other reason than our genuine need.

How much of what we buy is a genuine need? An opinion survey by the Harwood Group in the USA for the Merck Family Fund, entitled 'Yearning for Balance', found 82% of Americans agreeing that 'most of us buy and consume far more than we need; it's wasteful'. Another research study among 1,400 people, led by Dr Shaun Saunders of the University of Newcastle, New South Wales, found that the more materialistic an individual is, the more likely he or she is to be depressed, angry and dissatisfied with life. Dr Saunders remarked:

'Retail therapy provides a hollow form of fulfilment, something transient which is not compatible with a lifetime of happiness ... Someone else will always have more possessions, and this can lead to frustration and feelings of helplessness.'

𝝒 Exercise: Exactly why do you need that pair of shoes?

Each time you buy anything, ask yourself which need this fulfils. This can become a very interesting exercise, and will raise your level of awareness about the things that are controlling you. You have to be honest with yourself or this won't work in freeing you from being controlled by corporations or commerce. Suppose, for example, that after a shopping spree, you consider this question and one of your honest answers is that you are fulfilling a need of vanity, or that you have a need to keep up with friends, or that you need to compete with your peers. Well then, ask yourself, do you need this need?

If the answer is 'yes', then go ahead and feed the need. But at least know why you are consuming. Then you are in control. But it may also be that you recognise that you do not genuinely need a particular item, and so you can free yourself up from the tyranny of the consumer myth. The more you are able to free yourself from colluding with consumerism the lighter you will feel, and the less stressed you will be.

It is time to take back the control. We must stop being led like sheep into believing that we must accommodate every invention simply because it has been invented, or that we must obey every fashion and whim thought up by commercial interests to take our money from us. These are all endorsed by the media, of course, with the same intention of parting us from our hard-earned cash. In order that we are not reduced to robots or puppets controlled by state and commerce we have to begin to choose to opt out a little more. This is the secret of stress control.

We live in a situation like that in 'The Emperor's New Clothes'. We are all buying into something (in more ways than one!) that many of us suspect is deeply questionable, if not an outright deception, but somehow we fail to voice our misgivings lest we seem out of step, foolish or naïve. We have to find the courage of the small child to see the situation for what it is.

Who controls *your* mind?

I do not think we pay enough attention to the daily attempt to control our minds by the media, the advertising industry and the opinion makers in various walks of life. We take it all for granted, but if we were to visit another planet for a few months and then return to Earth, I think we would be amazed at the level of bombardment our minds receive from the various media, television, radio, newspapers, magazines, advertising posters, unsolicited mail, the internet and so on. I remember returning to London a few years ago after a month's holiday staying in the very peaceful and slow-paced countryside of Gran Canaria and feeling almost blown away by the billboards, posters and neon-lit words all screaming some sort of promotion at me as I journeyed through the streets towards home.

I think we should be more alarmed about this, perhaps even outraged. We are subjected to subliminal messages all through our waking hours; they are received by our unconscious minds and cause a lot of conflict and confusion below the surface of consciousness. In a recent television documentary about the advertising industry it was stated that we are exposed to 1,200 advertising messages per day. This creates anxiety, nervousness, jitteriness and fidgetiness. Any sensory input that we do not receive consciously and assimilate with interest makes us nervous, and has a destructive effect on our nervous systems, often leading to insomnia, a condition that is spreading like an epidemic in our civilisation.

Of course, I know that subliminal advertising is prohibited by law, but the overt messages all carry many subtle levels of meaning within them, which we all recognise but somehow collude with. When told: 'You must have this fantastic car, this amazing shampoo and conditioner, this soft, long toilet paper, this face cream, this particular soft drink, that particular make of jeans, this exotic holiday' and so on, the subtext is: 'It will make you feel successful, superior, valuable, acceptable – a member of the "In Group"; and if you cannot afford these things, or fail to acquire them for whatever reason, you are a failure, a nobody, a non-member of society, definitely not a member of any acceptable group.' Who says? Just ask yourself this question! Who exactly are the people telling you what to buy, wear and eat, and where to take your holidays? Are they people of superior judgement, exquisite taste and higher knowledge? Of course not! So, why allow them to influence you?

We are being dumped on

The point is that we are allowing ourselves to be dumped on continuously, and this is the really important point. So much of our current culture is just a great big dump! No wonder we are stressed; no wonder we are depressed; no wonder we are unfulfilled! We are dumped on continuously with other people's agendas and they are not friendly agendas, they are manipulative, self-interested agendas, not in the least bit concerned with our best interests. We are so used to it that we have become somewhat anaesthetised and desensitised to what is actually happening. We take it all in, pretty well uncensored, and obey. The way we are being controlled and manipulated is insidious and subtle, but those forces create a great deal of pressure on our minds and emotions. Those subliminal messages play on us, creating doubts and undermining our confidence, as well as promising counterfeit happiness.

We cannot eliminate these elements of our culture, but we can alter our reaction to them; we can be more aware of how much we allow them to influence our choices and our behaviour.

Counter measures

Do you really need to know all that depressing news and gossip churned out daily? Consuming it won't make any difference to the world's problems; it simply uses your time and energy for no good purpose. One of the ways to counteract the insidious influence of news and gossip is to cut down your consumption of media. Do not buy a newspaper every day and limit the amount of irrelevant items you consume from your TV, PC or tablet – give your mind a break!

A major part of the stress and tension we all feel is due to not spending enough time on inner reflection; our attention is focused too much on the outer world and not enough on the inner world of thoughts, feelings and imagination. This creates unbalance and much mental tiredness. So another part of our strategy has to be in rethinking our habits.

⋏ Exercise: Switch off from the outside world for a while

Instead of texting, reading the newspaper or a magazine whilst commuting, for example, close your eyes and imagine beautiful pictures: uplifting places that you know and love, or somewhere you create in your imagination. It can be somewhere in nature: a park, a garden, or a beach, or it could be a perfect room, filled with the objects and furniture you would love to have around you. Or just picture one beautiful and uplifting object like a waterfall, a tree, a flower, a crystal, a cross, a sunset, the sea, a rainbow – anything that brings you joy. You will be amazed how much less tired you will feel. Try it for a few days and start yourself on a new habit. This is the way to begin the practice of meditation.

Meditation is just an inner concentration of the mind; it slows your brainwaves and is stabilising and refreshing for the mind. Inner visualisation switches your mind from the word-orientated, logical left hemisphere of the brain, which is generally over-worked, to the creative right hemisphere.

Be patient with yourself

Don't worry if your mind will not stay on an inner image for long but keeps wandering off to thinking about the more mundane concerns of your life; just gently bring it back to your chosen visualisation each time you realise it has strayed. Do not become angry with yourself or with your mind, or despairing of your ability to concentrate. You have to train the mind in the same way as you would train a young animal. You must be very patient and gentle, and just keep on persevering. The more you practice this exercise, the more power you will gain over your mind.

The benefits of this greater control will ripple out into the rest of your life as you will find your powers of concentration improving and you will be able to focus on what *you* decide, rather than on what your mind decides to present to you. You'll become increasingly the master of your mind, and this means you will also have more control over negative or fearful thoughts. You will simply be able to say to your mind: 'No, thank you! I don't want to think that right now.' Get into the habit of practising uplifting visualisations whenever you have a little space, or when you are feeling particularly stressed and strained; it is a wonderful way to bring in more calm and to bring about a temporary disengagement with the outer world. This allows you to realign yourself and gain a fresh perspective.

Cut down on your screen time

Do not turn on the TV every day or every evening as an automatic reaction when you get home. Would that be so hard? If so, maybe you should question what this addiction really means, because staring at screens can become a sort of addiction.

Freeing yourself from too much TV or internet consumption gives you the chance to create your own world, your own atmosphere, rather than endlessly partaking of other people's ideas, conflicts or problems. There are so many alternatives to watching passively while other people perform and I really believe everyone would feel much better if they put limits on their screen time. It's important, also, for your general health to limit the time spent staring at TV or PC screens. There is more on this subject in the next chapter.

Apart from resting your senses from bombardment, think of the time it would free up for many other pursuits that perhaps you wish you could enjoy, like listening to your favourite music; reading all those novels, history books, autobiographies or self-development books you keep saying you want to; creating a beautiful garden or reorganising your home environment; learning another language; talking to your partner; listening to your children! Or just having time to drift and dream. It would give you back a sense of being more in control because you would not be consuming such a large portion of other people's agendas.

My suggestion is that you start by trying to have one day a week when you do not turn on your TV. Be firm with yourself and stick with it until you have broken the automatic habit of turning to your television to entertain you. It could be a different day each week but just stick with the principle that at least one day in the week the box does not go on! Then see if you can wean yourself away from spending large chunks of time on your PC or laptop. Just stop and think about what else you could be doing instead of passively looking at a screen! That might seem unthinkable, but give it a try and see if you feel that you have somehow reclaimed your life a little.

The same applies to the radio although I don't consider it such a negative influence because we have to exercise our imagination in the absence of visual images, which is important because it brings something from ourselves, from our creative mind, into the moment. But having the radio on in the background, and not really listening to it, is very tiring for your mind. Just giving your half-attention to anything is more fatiguing than giving your full attention and it is also disturbing for the nervous system, which cannot make full sense of what it is receiving.

Try to feel comfortable with silence. It is wonderfully restful for the mind. It is also amazing how many creative and imaginative thoughts arise in the absence of someone else's agenda. This is why so many people have their best ideas in the bath or shower –

it is often the only time in their day when they are removed from media and other people's input. Trust yourself to feel OK without constant outside help.

Of course, it takes a strong person to sail against the tide, but that is how we control our stress; by becoming stronger in our own convictions. As a result we are less likely to be coerced by somebody else's. We have to set our own agenda.

Just consider for a moment how much you are influenced by what is supposed to be fashionable, or the latest trend. A new word has been invented for this phenomenon: it is 'trendfear' – the anxiety that you are not keeping up with the cutting edge. Here again, it is important to be honest with yourself! How much do you worry that you have not managed to buy the latest version of your smartphone or tablet, or acquired the newest app, or even kept up-to-date with what is happening in the social media, or with any of the many gizmos, gadgets and accessories that are appearing faster than we can accommodate? Does it stress you that you have not seen the latest acclaimed film or play; not dined in one of the newest trendy restaurants; not been to the newly opened hip bar; not seen that popular TV programme or read the latest novel that is receiving so much media coverage, or studied that much talked about self-help book? Do you worry that you have not stuck to the latest fashionable diet, or started the exercise programme you know you 'should' do, or joined that yoga class that is so popular with certain film stars and other famous personalities. What a lot of baggage we carry around!

Do you see how we overload ourselves by being slaves to other people's control? I am not saying don't allow yourself to want things; just be sure that it is for the right reasons and not that you are keeping up with someone else's idea of what you 'should' be consuming.

All of this commercial pressure to have more, achieve more, keep up with the 'in crowd', and so on, just adds to the feelings of stress that we already have to contend with in our personal lives.

I see so many people – young and not so young, married and single, female and male – who are not happy because they are buying into someone else's idea of what they 'should' look like or what they 'should' be achieving or what kind of lover they 'should' have or what kind of person they think they 'ought' to be. Much of this pressure to do and be what is not really right for them as individuals is coming from society's messages via the media, advertising and so on. But those sources are not the slightest bit interested in your well-being – they are interested in the health of their balance sheets, their profits. Remember that! Realise also that the level of consumption that is encouraged by commercial advertising is actually unsustainable and so contributes not only to personal stress but to global problems as well.

Kevin Costner once said in a TV interview: 'It seems as if the world is asleep at the wheel!' I absolutely agree with him. We really must wake up. We have to develop more confidence in ourselves, and set our own agendas. Do not allow a particular brand to tell you that you must possess it. What madness is this?

Our insecurities are triggered by commercial propaganda

The marketplace exploits your insecurities and fears by making you feel inadequate, that you are not good enough, inducing you to buy more and more to feel OK. When our insecurities are triggered, they are in control. Therefore we need to check out frequently which part of ourselves is really in control. Is it the child within that feels little and powerless and who needs an outside authority to set the agenda; or the part that feels unattractive and the wrong shape; or is it the internal parent voice telling you that you are worthless, stupid or no good? We all have many negative sub-personalities such as the 'inner critic', the 'insecure child', the 'unattractive adolescent' that clamour for control within us, but if we can recognise them for what they are we can reduce their influence.

Strengthen your power

When one of your insecurities, or negative self-talk, has been triggered, and you're feeling insecure or anxious, call up in your mind's eye a picture of yourself at some time when you felt really good about yourself; when you felt truly what you might call your 'Best Self'. Then affirm to yourself that this is who you are. This is your true potential, waiting to be realised at any moment. If you've been there once there's no reason why you can't be there again at any time you choose. Keep affirming that picture and the knowledge that you absolutely know this is who you can be, who you are, in fact. We so often put blocks in our own way and trip ourselves up or undermine ourselves with our negative self-talk and doubts. But if you keep affirming inwardly that picture of you at your best, as your sublime and most powerful self, you will reinforce that image. Just keep seeing yourself in the situation where you knew you were your true self. Whatever we tell ourselves on a regular basis sinks into our subconscious mind and becomes what we believe. Strengthen your power by reinforcing your best self-image, over and over, many times a day; then when you need a powerful boost of self-confidence that image will immediately spring to mind and remind you of who you really are.

Live lightly in the world

Another way to approach the consumer society, and to distance oneself a little from its negative influences, is to take the attitude promoted by many Eastern philosophies:

'Be in the world but not of the world.'

This does not mean you have to become a recluse, join a commune of self-sufficiency, or even live way out of the city in the middle of nowhere; it means changing the focus of your attention. It means concentrating your energy, enthusiasm, imagination and interest on all that is not part of the materialistic, corporate world, more often than perhaps you do at present. As I have already said, try to limit how much commercialism you take into your brain and how much space it occupies on your agenda and include more that is artistic, imaginative, spiritual, soulful, natural and free. Give equal weight and value to these other aspects of life. Practice distancing yourself from the commercial world and its dictates. Release your attachment to the things that can cause you stress. By this I do not mean you have to stop doing anything you were doing before – just release your attachment to it, your dependence on it and identification with it.

Identify with the eternal and lasting rather than with the transient

Greater serenity and 'centredness' are achieved by beginning to identify with the things that are more eternal, substantial and less transitory than what is on offer in the marketplace; and by spending more time thinking about, learning about and engaging with those aspects of life. This links back into what I said in Chapter 2 about your own truths and values. It is on this level that you find peace and happiness of a more sustaining kind, and it creates a counterbalance to our 'throw away' culture; it will give you more resources with which to tackle everyday life. If you can slowly develop a greater degree of non-attachment to the material world you will feel an increased calm in the face of problems.

This is not a rejection of anything, it is simply a shift of position so that your relationship with the transient becomes more distant, more disengaged, more detached and freer. It is in letting go that we can find our own release.

One of my personal philosophies is not to become too attached to, or depend too much on, anything that can be taken away from me; not to rely too much on something that someone else, or circumstances, can suddenly remove. The optimum thought here is: *'not to rely too much'*; it is the *'too much'* that needs emphasising. Obviously we have to depend on certain things provided by others, but try to gain your most valuable support and strength from things that cannot easily be taken away. For example, I gain my support from, among other things (which includes my friends and the people I love), my inner life of meditation and thinking, my enjoyment of reading and writing, as well as music and poetry, art and beauty in any form, a beautiful garden, wonderful architecture or a fabulous sunset, watching inspiring films or documentaries; as well as simple creative pursuits like arranging flowers, cooking a delicious meal or arranging a room artistically; and above all, I derive great joy from being surrounded by the natural world in all its myriad forms, at the beach, in a wood, walking through fields or just around a city garden square. Nature is always there to uplift you and inspire you when you open yourself up to those influences.

I do believe there is much truth in the adage that 'the best things in life are free', and this is especially true with regard to all the natural wonders of the world. Take some time to contemplate the natural beauty around you. Recognise that we are always in nature; we don't necessarily have to make special trips out into the countryside. Just look up at the sky more often, its changing shapes and colours are a wonderful sight for sore eyes! Let the vastness of it transport you for a moment or two and enlarge your perspective on your world.

Look at trees with your full attention and really see them as you walk down the street or in local parks. It's important to take the time to stand back and stare in awe and wonder at the magnificence, complexity and beauty of it all, and in gratitude at what we have been given. Research by Tokyo's Nippon Medical School found that people who spend time walking in a forest or park have significantly lower levels of stress hormones than people walking in urban surroundings. Another study reported in the *European Journal of Applied Physiology* showed that people spending time immersed in nature had lower blood pressure. This enhances the 'biophilia' theory that humans find natural surroundings instinctively more calming. Other research has discovered that people whose flats overlook gardens have lower levels of stress hormones than those whose apartments have views only of other buildings.

Remember the words of the famous poem *Leisure* by W.H. Davies:

'What is this life if, full of care, we have no time to stand and stare?'

⊼ Exercise: Wonder in the glories of nature

Nourish and uplift yourself by standing and staring as often as you can! Walk in parks and admire and appreciate the creative work that goes into making them beautiful for you to enjoy. Walk along the riverbank or beside a canal and discover a new and amazing world of 'water people' and water wildlife. Also, of course, try to get away from the concrete city and immerse yourself in the deep countryside as much as possible or at the beach and the sea – feast your senses and reconnect with the bigger picture.

Pioneer researcher Dr Hans Selye, whom I mentioned in Chapter 1, wrote in his book, *The Stress of Life:*

> *'The most harmonious and mysterious creations are those of Nature; and to my mind, it is the highest cultural aim of the professional scientist to interpret that so that others may share in their enjoyment ... there is an equanimity and a peace of mind which can be achieved only through contact with the sublime.'*

Instead of seeing yourself as a citizen of the materialist society, try thinking of yourself as a citizen of the natural world, which means everything on the planet that is natural and beautiful, and not man-made. Claim your place within all that miraculous beauty. Many of our current problems arise from the fact that we have forgotten we are creatures of nature. When we put ourselves outside nature, then we can exploit and destroy it. In my opinion we are identifying with the wrong side! Yes, we are all responsible to a greater or lesser degree for our current world but if we could step back and observe it all a little more objectively we might live more lightly in it.

Treat it all as a joke, or a game not to be taken too seriously, that you pack up at the end of the day and can begin again in the morning if you choose. Learn to laugh at it. Consume it lightly but don't let it consume you. Don't be controlled by the marketplace. The marketplace doesn't care about you, it is out to exploit you. Of course we need the marketplace for transactions to take place, but that's all – that's all!

American university professor of business administration, Ralph Estes, says in his book, *Tyranny of the Bottom Line: Why Corporations Make Good People Do Bad Things* (1995 published by Berrett-Koehler) that business is a system originally created to serve the public interest but it has gone astray through an unbalanced focus on profit, a 'perverse score-keeping system that measures a company's effects on stockholders but not on employees, customers or the larger community.' Commerce has forgotten its original intentions and *raison d'etre*, so do not identify with it too completely. See it merely as a convenience, not the last resort. Keep your distance. We take it too seriously. The marketplace is not the final destination. Remember the words of the poet William Wordsworth:

> *'The world is too much with us; late and soon,*
> *Getting and spending, we lay waste our powers.'*

Can you imagine how differently the world stage would look if we prioritised inner development above outer, material growth, if we valued wisdom more than wealth? We could do it. Humankind could decide to change the focus. Who says we must worship material wealth? Why not worship natural resources or beauty? Why not say that the winners in life are the ones with the most beautiful countries and the least damaged natural habitats? Does it sound so crazy? We could certainly do with a shift in balance towards that other side.

🯄 Exercise: Visualising a different world

- Create an inner picture of two roads; one that is full of the activity of the marketplace, the average high street; and the other a country road typical of those in France, bordered by trees with fields stretching away into the distance.
- See yourself walking down the country road. That is the true path of your life because you are a part of the natural world. Think of the other one as a place you visit from time to time as you choose. Always you return at the close of day to the place of tranquillity, in nature and peace. See these roads as a metaphor for your journey through life.

- Hold those two roads in your imagination and get used to seeing them as the two possibilities of your life. You can travel down one or the other, as you choose, but you must always come home to the tranquil road.
- Now create in your imagination a picture of a beautiful sanctuary, it could be a house, a hut, a garden or a temple – somewhere you would like to be, that would soothe and refresh you.
- Place your sanctuary somewhere along the country road and know that this is a place into which you can withdraw whenever you feel in need of peace and solace; it is your natural home, the special place within yourself to which you can return regularly. This will provide the balance to the marketplace.
- Never stay too long in the marketplace, for that is what stresses you! Return at frequent intervals to your sanctuary. But, of course, it is your choice.

In *Siddhartha*, Hermann Hesse writes:

'Within you there is a stillness and sanctuary to which you can retreat at any time and be yourself.'

This sanctuary is an inner awareness of comfort; an inner feeling of ease that cannot be disturbed by turmoil or distress. Through the practice of visualisation and relaxation, it is possible for everyone to experience this state within. It is also the state that is experienced in meditation.

You might like to copy out, and carry around as a reminder, the following injunction from the wise spiritual teacher, Lao-Tzu; the supposed author of the *Tao Te Ching*:

> *'Manifest plainness,*
> *Embrace simplicity,*
> *Reduce selfishness,*
> *Have few desires.'*

Chapter 4

Technology and stress

In the past few decades we have witnessed the most amazing advances in technology, and yet all these wonders don't seem to make us any happier. In fact, according to the World Health Organisation, depression now affects just over 120 million people worldwide. This may not seem a very large percentage of the world's total population, but it is still a rather staggering figure. We have so much more to occupy and amuse us than previous generations and yet this appears not to increase our happiness. What is the problem?

I believe it is connected to what has been discussed in the previous chapter; all of our technology, gadgetry and diverting gizmos take us away from ourselves. We are overly distracted. Distracted from what exactly? Well, in my view, we are distracted away from the things that really matter; the things which, in fact, can make us happy.

I shall return to this theme a little later on, but for now, I want to focus on the practicalities of interacting with technology, and how to diminish its adverse effects.

Mobile (or cell) phones and smartphones

Mobile phones, also known as a cellular phones or cell phones, and new generation smartphones, emit low levels of radio frequency radiation in the microwave range while being used. It is well known that high levels of radio frequency radiation can produce biological damage through heating effects (this is how a microwave oven is able to cook food). However, it is not known to what extent, if at all, lower levels of this electromagnetic radiation might cause adverse health effects in users of mobile phones. There is ongoing research into this important question, and the findings so far are inconclusive, although there has recently appeared some evidence that long-term mobile phone use could be implicated in the development of brain tumours and salivary gland tumours. In 2004, a 750-people study by Sweden's Karolinska Institute found that using a mobile phone for ten years or more increases the risk of ear tumours by four times. On 31 May 2011, the World Health Organisation confirmed that mobile phone use may represent a long-term health risk, classifying mobile phone radiation as a "carcinogenic hazard" and "possibly carcinogenic to humans" after a team of scientists reviewed peer-review studies on cell phone safety.

In 2000, an independent expert group in the UK, chaired by Sir William Stewart, produced a report titled "Mobile Phones and Health" which has become known as the Stewart Report. This report advised caution due to uncertainties in the biological evidence, and recommended that children should only use mobile phones in emergencies. This is because children's brains are still developing and their skulls are thinner, making it easier for the radio waves to penetrate them. Also, if children start using cell phones at a young age their cumulative lifetime use will be higher than for adults. This advice was accepted by the Department of Health and continues to be the advice of the UK Health Protection Agency. The Agency recommends that excessive use of mobile phones by children should be discouraged.

There is also concern about the long-term effect of the numerous 'hotspots' around the globe, providing Wi-Fi connections to the internet from almost anywhere you happen to find yourself; this has been termed 'electrosmog'. Parents are worried that Wi-Fi electromagnetic fields in schools, as well as cell phone masts in playgrounds, might pose a health risk to their children. The research studies so far do not indicate any serious health risk from exposure to this low level radiation. However, the International Agency for Research on Cancer (IARC) has classified Wi-Fi radiation (radio frequency electromagnetic fields) as a Class 2B carcinogen in the same risk category as lead, the pesticide DDT and petrol exhausts; therefore, it is not considered entirely harmless. It is recommended that you switch off your home Wi-Fi at night. It is also considered essential by the scientific community that research continues to evaluate the long-term exposure to these hazards, as they have only been around for a comparatively short time.

Steps that can be taken to reduce the risk from radiation from technology

Experts say that it is particularly difficult to predict the long-term impact of a product that is just two decades old, especially as many users only began using them in the past five years. However, below is a list of preventative measures you can take.

1. **Keep use short:** Almost all the experts agree that the best step is to keep mobile phone conversations short and to a minimum.

2. **Use hands-free kits:** Many believe that hands-free kits reduce the risk by cutting the amount of electromagnetic radiation entering the brain.

3. **Use external aerials:** As the radiation is emitted from the aerial, using an external aerial means that it is as far away from the head as possible.

4. **Use phones with a long talk time:** It is believed that phones with a long talk time are more efficient and produce less powerful emissions.

5. **Restrict phone use in the car:** Try not to use mobile phones in the car as stronger radiation is required to penetrate the car body. Avoid use in completely enclosed metallic environments like elevators as the radiation cannot escape and has nowhere to go but into your body.

6. **Use a bag:** Do not carry your phone in a pocket close to your body, especially near to your heart or your reproductive organs. Carry your cell phone in a separate bag as much as possible, or at least in the outside pocket of an overcoat or jacket.

7. **Turn off your Wi-Fi:** As a precaution against the cumulative radiation effect of Wi-Fi, it is advisable to switch off your home Wi-Fi at night.

The amount of radiation a human body will absorb from a cell phone is called the SAR, which stands for "specific absorption rate". The lower the SAR the less radiation will be absorbed. Governments in different countries have set limits on the allowable SAR. In North America the SAR limit for mobile phones used by the public is 1.6 watts/kilogram (W/kg) averaged over one gram of body tissue. The European Standard is 2.0 watts/kilogram (W/kg) averaged over ten grams of body tissue. Different makes of mobile phone have differing rates of radiation. In order to compare relative radiation of different cell phones, you can only compare phones using the same standard of measurement.

Cell phone radiation charts that compare SAR levels of different makes can be found online. You can also purchase radiation shields for your cell phone by researching online manufacturers, although some shields have been shown to provide little or no protection after independent tests took place. Therefore, when searching for a radiation shield it is important to check the research on the degree of protection offered. Tests conducted by the ABC show *20/20* in the US, found that some of the country's most popular cell phones can (depending on how they are held) exceed the radiation limit.

Possible consequences of radiation exposure

- Headaches
- Unusual fatigue
- Nervousness and restlessness
- High blood pressure
- Sleep disorder
- Weakness of concentration
- Exhaustion
- Allergies
- Hormonal dysfunction
- Accelerated aging of the skin
- Weakening of the immune system

If you are suffering unduly from any of these symptoms you should seriously consider reducing your use of your cell phone or smartphone, as a precaution. It was thought that the new smartphones which have so many more features would emit higher amounts of radiation, but some research indicates that this is not the case, and that in fact some smartphones emit lower radiation levels than the older, lower feature models. However, it is sensible practice to discover the SAR of your particular phone, which can be researched online by typing in 'cell phone radiation'. Moreover, it has been reported that not all smartphone manufacturers are making the effort to design phones with lower emissions, and the industry is reported to be lobbying the regulation agencies to loosen the radiation limits. Therefore, it is wise to be vigilant on this subject as your long-term health could be at risk.

Cordless phones

Cordless phones operate in a similar way to mobile phones, that is, by using radio signals to communicate between a handset and a base station. However, the Health Protection Agency has stated that cordless phones and their base stations have output powers much too low for exposures to exceed internationally accepted guidelines and the HPA does not consider there are particular safety issues with their use. The only caution they advise is that you do not sleep with the base station beside your bed, close to your head.

Personal computers and laptops

Our PCs and laptops have become increasingly indispensable tools in assisting us with the myriad processes of daily life. However, sitting for long periods of time at your PC or laptop stresses the physical body. The human body is designed to move, not to stay still in a relatively static posture. Bearing this in mind it is wise to take regular breaks from sitting in front of your screens. You should get up and move around every two hours of computer work, or at least stretch your arms and legs, circle your shoulders (other exercises are described in Chapter 9) and have a good yawn. If you can, jog up and down on the spot, run up a flight of stairs, or go for a short walk outside in the fresh air to increase your circulation and deepen your breathing.

It has been found that people's concentration begins to falter and mistakes are made after two hours of continuous focused screen work; so a physical break where you move your body will help restore your concentration when you return to your screen.

Coupled with the fact that our bodies are not well served by sitting still for much of the day, another problem is also that too many continuous hours spent keying in to your computer can cause a debilitating condition called Repetitive Strain Injury (RSI), also known as overuse injury or upper limb disorder. It begins as mild pain in the arms, shoulders, wrists, elbows or fingers, and should not be ignored, even if the pain is slight. If the intensity of the pain increases this indicates further damage is taking place, and you must seek medical advice. The pain is the result of the overuse of muscles in repetitive movements, which causes inflammation in the muscles, and can lead to long-term problems and even loss of use in hands and arms. Our children are now falling victim to this condition as a result of constant texting, with pain mostly in their thumbs and fingers. If you, or your children, do experience these kinds of pains – which are also associated with carpal tunnel syndrome and 'tennis elbow' – it is essential that you seek the advice of a specialist. There are doctors who specialise in the treatment of this condition, and treatment requires not just resting the muscles, but also specialised exercises and stretches to ensure the muscles do not atrophise, and to strengthen adjacent muscles.

There have been recent reports about this condition also badly affecting workers in the Far East who manufacture our smartphones, tablets, laptops and so on. They are allegedly required to work extremely long hours performing the same repetitive movements the entire time they are at work, and it has been reported that many workers are losing the use of their hands and arms as they are not receiving the medical care they need. Many other workers engaged in repetitive movements such as hairdressers, musicians, checkout counter operators, chicken pluckers, postal workers, construction and agricultural workers and, long ago, Morse code operators, have suffered from this condition. Fortunately, however, it is now better understood and better treated than in previous generations. Nevertheless, it is important not to ignore the first signs of overusing your muscles such as strong aches or pain, and to then rest those muscles or change to a different type of movement using different muscles, as well as seeking medical opinion.

It is especially important to ensure that your chair is well designed to support your body at your PC station, and that your chair and desk are the correct height in relation to each other. Badly designed furniture and bad postures will take their toll on your physical body causing backache, tension and pain in shoulders and upper back muscles, headaches, lower back pain, and RSI, all of which are the result of wrong postures or overuse.

Use of laptops

People using laptops often balance them on beds, on their laps (as the name implies) or on sofas that force them to sit in awkward positions with their body twisted in unsymmetrical angles. This way of working on your laptop can stress and strain the body as it is pulled out of its true alignment. Over time these postures can result in seriously debilitating physical problems that will often need months of physiotherapy treatment to put right. Consequently, take care how you position your body when using your laptop and do not twist it into uncomfortable and awkward postures (see figure 1).

It is important that the height of your desk allows your forearms to be parallel to the floor while you are using a keyboard. This should be positioned to allow your wrists to be also kept parallel to the floor to avoid undue strain. Your wrists should not be bent upwards, dropped downwards or deviated inwards or outwards. All of those undesirable positions contribute to RSI and other

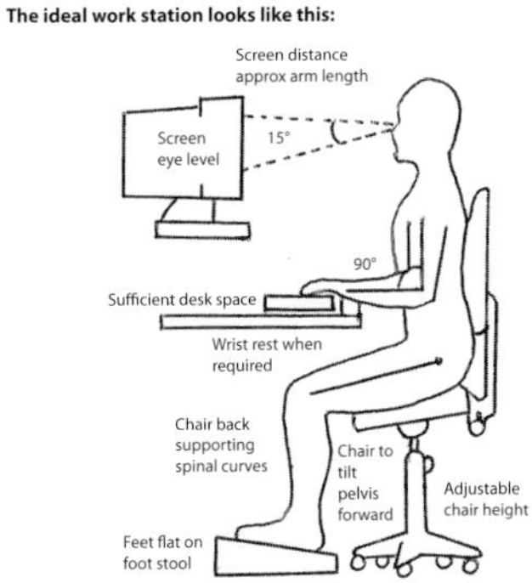

The ideal work station looks like this:

Screen distance
approx arm length

Screen
eye level   15"

90°

Sufficient desk space

Wrist rest when
required

Chair back
supporting
spinal curves

Chair to
tilt
pelvis
forward

Adjustable
chair height

Feet flat on
foot stool

Figure 1: The ideal positions for your body at a workstation or desk (© Wendy Chalmers Mill)

disorders such as carpal tunnel syndrome, tenosynovitis and tendonitis. When sitting at your desk your elbows should be bent at about 90 degrees and they should be in line with your shoulders. There should be sufficient room for you to put your legs comfortably under the desk.

A good chair will be designed so that all its component parts move independently, enabling it to be adjusted to suit your shape, size and height. It should fully support your spine, especially in your lower back. Placing a small, firm cushion in the small of the back can give extra support if you are suffering from backache. Specifically designed posture cushions are available from a number of sources, and these are also recommended for use in your car if you frequently spend many hours driving. (See Useful Addresses.) When sitting at your workstation or desk, both feet should be able to rest flat on the floor. If your legs are dangling it causes strain on your lower back and you should therefore introduce a footstool or some kind of support under your feet so that they are resting on something. Your knees should be bent at an angle of about 90 degrees so that your heels are resting just under your knees. Try not to cross your legs as this impairs circulation (exacerbating varicose veins) and twists the spine, which puts a strain on your back muscles. The seat depth should comfortably support your legs from hip to knee without putting pressure on the middle of the thigh.

There should be enough spring or give in the chair to support your body and to eliminate shock through your spine. However, it should not be so soft that it allows your pelvis to sink into it. Ideally, there should be a swivel and a five-castor base to allow the chair to move freely. Adjustable armrests may be helpful, but are not absolutely necessary (see figure 2).

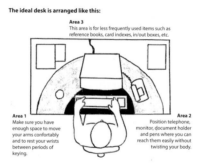

The ideal desk is arranged like this:

Area 3
This area is for less frequently used items such as reference books, card indexes, in/out boxes, etc.

Area 1
Make sure you have enough space to move your arms confortably and to rest your wrists between periods of keying.

Area 2
Position telephone, monitor, document holder and pens where you can reach them easily without twisting your body.

Figure 2: The ideal desk arrangement (© Wendy Chalmers Mill)

The equipment on top of your desk should be arranged so that you avoid asymmetrical postures. This means that the height of your VDU screen, or monitor, should be at eye level and directly in front of you. The screen should be at an arm's length from where you are sitting. Your keyboard should also be directly in front of your body so that your joints can remain in as neutral a position as possible. If your body is symmetrical, with your spine straight and head held straight, you will feel less fatigued and it will minimise aches and pains as you will not be putting undue strain on your body. If your work does involve a lot of screen work, take note of these additional points:

- Keep the screen clean.

- The screen brightness and contrast should be adjusted in accordance with the lighting conditions. Glare and reflection must be minimised. Ideally, the screen should be positioned at a 90 degree angle to the light source. Lighting should also be positioned to eliminate reflections.

- Avoid the colour white as much as possible, as it is the most reflective colour: for example, white walls, white desks, white clothes, white paper.

- Be aware that glass panelling and the glass in picture frames also cause reflections.

- Document holders are very helpful when you are keying from copy as they minimise the need for awkward movements of your head and eyes. The ideal one is hinged like an anglepoise lamp and can be positioned to the side of the screen at the same height and distance.

- Take care about securing all cables and flexes required for power to computers, printers, photocopiers etc. Cables should not encroach on leg space and should be taped or bridged on the floor to avoid tripping.

We need to ensure that technology is more helpful than harmful to our lives. If used wisely our machines, gizmos and gadgets can enhance daily living, but when we become enslaved to them, or do not use them sensibly, they tend to undermine the quality of life. As outlined above, how we engage with our technology in a physical sense can have a negative effect on our physical body; but, in addition to this, when technology takes us away from real life, for too long, then we must question what is actually happening to us as human beings.

The real danger in technology

When we have no time to play with or read to our children, or when we take them for walks in the park but spend most of the time on our cell phones rather than engaging with them; or when we would prefer to spend time with friends on Facebook, or any other social networking site, rather than with friends in real time; when we spend our leisure time sitting still looking at our computer screens, having spent the working week doing just that. Well, isn't something wrong?

Technology is stressing us because it does not allow us enough time to get out into the real world and have fun, take exercise, play or experience any number of real-life pleasures. But it is not the fault of the technology, it is our fault because we give ourselves to it! We give it too much time and importance in our lives and this is where the real danger lies.

People seem to think there is always going to be something more interesting appearing on their smartphone or tablet screen than what is actually in front of them, even when out with friends or partners. It's like a drug that we can't stop consuming. This is the addictive aspect of technology and the insidious grip it has on us. We need to bring our interest back into the real world and find the delights in real time, in the here and now, giving our full attention to whatever is in front of us in the moment. We are forgetting how to enjoy our world, and so we keep looking for happiness in our technology, but it is an illusion which is unlikely to give us lasting satisfaction. There are actually many wonderful things right under our nose but we don't see them because we are distracted. We have to learn to leave 'technology' at home (or at least switched off) more often than we are doing at this moment in time. Then we'll regain our joy and our enthusiasm for the simple things and our imaginations will be freed up from other people's input. We need to look up from our screens and get back in touch with life, real life, not cyber life! We need to wake up to what we are allowing to happen to us. How can we be happy in the moment when we are not fully present in it?

We are fascinated with technology, but the fascination can turn into fixation if we fail to balance our lives sensibly. We are allowing life to narrow down into too much cyber, or virtual life, and we need to address our real-life needs more consciously.

It may seem as if I am against technology, but actually my concern is not with 'technology' but with our addiction to it! It's like the quote that is so often misunderstood: *the love of money is the route of all evil*. It is not *money* that is the route of all evil – no, it is the 'love' of money that takes one down that slippery path. Similarly, it is not 'technology' that is the problem, rather it is our 'love' of technology that is the problem. I believe that our addiction to technology is leading us down very dangerous paths because it is taking over and gaining too much control over human beings.

Doctors are warning that future generations highly addicted to technology will suffer both physical and mental health problems. Recent medical studies have shown that the brain's reaction to computer games is similar to that seen with drugs and alcohol. The work of Dr Aric Sigman, psychologist, broadcaster and best-selling author, along with other researchers, has found a link between time spent in front of screens and physical problems such as: obesity, high cholesterol and high blood pressure, inattentiveness and a decline in maths and reading ability, as well as sleep disorders.

Technology also stresses us mentally because our minds are too frequently split between what is in front of us and what is continuously appearing on our screens. This divided attention is very tiring and irritating for the mind. So, I simply caution you to keep technology in its place, to control its influence on your life and to take care of your physical well-being in relation to its use, as I have outlined above.

I'd finally like to return to the point I made at the beginning of this chapter. If we allow technology to distract us away from real life for too much of the time we are limiting our experiences. If you spend a large percentage of your day/week/month/year looking at your technology, you are not fully 'here'. This means you could be losing a huge amount of your life! If you are texting, or surfing the internet, or looking up friends' activities on one of the social media sites, you are mentally somewhere else and if you are not mentally 'here' then you are missing out on the present moment, which is the only moment that you have. You can't do life in the future, or the past – or in someone else's world on the internet – you have to experience your life right here, right now. You can't make your life enjoyable, happy or rewarding if you're not here! This is why we are not any happier, and in some cases are much unhappier, today than in previous generations, because we can't make the present moment happy if we're not in it!

Many people experience a 'low' or depressed feeling when they switch off from their computers or laptops, or even their phone screens, because they have been experiencing an artificial 'high' in cyberspace. It's similar to the 'downer' experience when the artificial 'high' of alcohol or drugs has worn off. Coming back into the actual world can be a shock, because you come back to yourself and there is no-one else entertaining or distracting you. But the real world holds so much that is interesting, amazing and inspiring if you really look. You have to be present to find the exquisite moment. We keep thinking that the happiness we seek is somewhere else, in someone else's world, or is going to happen tomorrow or in the future, or maybe at the party at the weekend. You may think your life is boring, but that is because you're not trying to make it interesting. Stop looking down and texting your friend. Look up and look out at our beautiful world. You have to find interesting things in real life, not in cyberspace or in someone else's world on your tablet screen!

When you are truly in the present moment you will find that your stresses melt away because there is usually nothing you can't cope with. It is often things from the future (which haven't happened yet) that we mostly worry and stress about, not what is here now in the present. Actually, the present moment is the only moment that is real, and it is only in the present moment that you can do anything, or make a difference to your life. You can't act in the future until the future becomes the present and you can't change the past so you might as well let go of it and be here **now**.

The scientist, educator and spiritual teacher Rudolf Steiner once said to his audience: 'Miracles happen every day, you just don't see them.' The reason we don't see them is because we are not here – we are distracted.

⚔ Exercise: The here and now

Spend regular time focusing only on what is around you in the moment, and see if you can find at least one miracle every day. If you do this, it will uplift your life and take your mind away from worries and stresses.

For more information on the topic, I urge you to read the marvellous book by Eckhart Tolle entitled *The Power of Now* (2001 published by Hodder).

Chapter 5

Take control of your agenda

'Stress as overload' is a definition most people relate to and grasp immediately. One way of better understanding the phenomenon of 'overload' is to imagine yourself carrying a number of items on a tray, which you can manage perfectly well until someone comes along and loads a few more items on top of what is already there. The tray now becomes quite heavy but you can still cope by tightening your muscles and bracing yourself. However, imagine two more people appearing, each placing an extra, extremely heavy item on top of everything else. Suddenly you are beyond the limit of your strength, and you drop the lot! The relevant point is that you were carrying most of the things quite easily; it was only when the last one or two were added that you dropped everything. And this is what happens in our lives. We can cope happily up to a certain point, with a certain amount; but if pushed beyond the limit of our resources too frequently, or for too long, we can suddenly become incapable of coping with anything at all. We drop the lot!

The image of overload is easy to understand and cannot easily be denied. Too much overloading, whether physical or mental, and something has to give. This is a very good description of what is happening to many people when they say they feel stressed. They are being pushed beyond their limit; this means, overloaded beyond the limit of the resources they have available to respond to, and deal comfortably with, whatever is being demanded of them.

Too much on your agenda?

So many people feel their agendas are overloaded: this is something I hear all the time. Why? And who is loading them up? Why are we piling more and more onto ourselves? We need to ask this question; but we also need to be helped to offload. This is an essential key to our greater well-being. If you put too much onto your agenda you may find that even the easy things feel difficult because you are overloaded. Too much is too much, whatever its nature!

People often say to me, 'What I am doing is not very difficult, so I shouldn't make a fuss about feeling stressed.' Well no, it may not be difficult, but it can still be too much! You only have so many hours in a day and it is important to become clear about how you want to spend those hours. A lot of what we do and think can be classed as clutter, trivia or unnecessary. When I say unnecessary, I mean this in terms of your true goals and aims; the same applies to the other two words: clutter and trivia. If we spend time on things which will not advance us towards our goals and objectives, then we will always feel frustrated and stressed because we will not have enough time left for the things that really matter – that will take us to where we feel successful and fulfilled. If you have unnecessary things in your life, you will have to spend time on their maintenance and upkeep, which is time taken away from the necessary and important things. Or, if you neglect them you'll feel guilty about the neglect, and this will be another stress to carry around. So whichever way you look at it, you do not want unnecessary things!

Clearing to move forwards

A wise spiritual healer I know says that you must always clear to move forwards. Often the reason we can't move on, or feel blocked, is that we have not thought enough about clearing out, or eliminating, some of the clutter and excess baggage we carry, both in our outer, material life and in our inner thoughts and feelings.

Spend some time thinking about what you want in your life and what you do not want or need any longer. Remember that it is impossible to have more of what you want if your agenda is still crammed full with a great deal of what you don't want!

In order to become more in control of our own agendas, the first thing that is necessary is to give ourselves permission to jettison all the stuff that is not really of our choosing; things that we are not really too comfortable about, that we don't really want but which we have somehow been persuaded that we *should* (there's that word again!) accommodate. Try to picture in your imagination how your life would look, and feel, if you had a good clear out and got rid of the things you think you 'should' have, but don't want.

Only you can know what you'd be better off without, but it is important to get rid of the 'stuff' that is bogging you down to no avail. Once you've cleared some space, you can then think about what you'd really like to have there, or whether perhaps you simply enjoy having the space.

It's important to remember that it is, after all, *your* agenda, and so you are entitled to be in charge of it! It is also important to work out just what stops you from doing what you want to do. When you are being true to yourself, rather than complying with some idea of what you 'should' do, or be, much stress is released. I came across this apt little message recently on a calendar aimed at 'Women Who Do Too Much':

'We are not really asked to live anyone else's life. All we have to do is live our own, and that seems to be quite enough, indeed.'

Of course, it is an obvious statement, but just seeing it stated baldly like that started me thinking about how much other people's lives encroach on our own; how much time we perhaps spend thinking or gossiping about other people's problems, which won't make the slightest difference to them and certainly won't take us nearer to our own goals!

☓ Exercise: Spring-clean your life!

Take an overview of your life and imagine you are about to have a huge spring-clean! How would you go about it? It is certainly not usual to get so carried away with the impulse to spring-clean that we throw everything out and buy all our possessions anew. That would be ridiculous. However, deciding to let go of some of the stuff we have been hanging onto can feel such a relief! It makes you feel so much lighter. And once you let some things go, you can appreciate the value of the good and necessary things. But when you are cluttered up, you can't see anything clearly, you just feel overloaded by everything – even the good things.

How often do we agree to meet up with people in whom we are not terribly interested? Or how much time do we spend talking about famous personalities in the news and people we encounter through the media, whom we don't even know and will probably never meet? How much time and attention do we give to thinking about other people's successes or failures, what others should, or should not, do? How much emotion is spent on worrying about friends and family or other people's opinions? And on it goes. This is energy and time taken away from our own lives. So just take a moment to say to yourself:

'I only have to live my life.'

And repeat it regularly a number of times every day. Then give up trying to live other people's lives for them!

Reviewing your agenda – 1

Spend a little time mentally reviewing your agenda. Try to get in touch with the things that you really do not want to do or the attitudes you project that are not really your own, or the beliefs you pretend to subscribe to which perhaps get you into situations you'd rather not be in. Make a list of these things that you want to be rid of: the baggage that is weighing you down. You may wish to organise it in two columns, one headed 'Outer Agenda' for things in your outer life that you would like to jettison, and the other headed 'Inner Stuff' for your attitudes, thoughts, fears, beliefs that trip you up and keep you un-free. Alternatively, you may just have one continuous list. Then mentally sideline them every day.

The way to do this is:

● Look at the list, or the two columns, a number of times a day and as you focus on each item say to yourself:

'This is not me. This is not part of my life.'

● Have the list(s) beside you on the seat of the car as you drive to work or as you return home after the school run. Each time you stop at a traffic light, glance at one item on your list and repeat the sentences as above:

'This is not me. This is not part of my life.'

● Or mentally repeat this exercise on your journey into work by train, bus or bicycle, or while out walking the dog. Choose the most urgent to focus on first and gradually work down the list.

- Do the same at regular breaktimes during the day: at a coffee break, at lunch time, at a tea break, on the train on the way home or in the bus or car, in the supermarket queue or waiting to go into the cinema – anywhere you suddenly have a little space. Affirm to yourself what is not you and what you do not want! Just repeat:

  'This is not me. This is not part of my life.'

- Go through the exercise last thing at night before you go to sleep. Focus on the most important points so that the thoughts are carried into your subconscious mind as you fall asleep.

You have to say the phrases in the present tense to convince your subconscious mind that the statements are true right now even though they are not. If you say them in the future tense, for example, 'This will not be me for much longer,' your subconscious cannot know when the message is going to apply, which will confuse it, and so it will be disregarded. You have to start believing it right now.

The frequent repetition of this exercise will create strong new neural pathways in your brain and will convince your subconscious mind of the truth in the statements. The subconscious mind believes what it is told; rather like a child it does not discriminate or judge the material it is fed, and so if you feed in positive statements it will believe them and that will have a powerful effect on your life. You will then discover that your external behaviour begins to alter in a way that more truly demonstrates who you are and what you want.

Once you start to alter your inner conditioning many of these things will just take care of themselves. When your inner attitude changes a lot of things will just fall away, or you will simply lose interest in the things that were not really necessary. For example:

- You may suddenly realise that you have stopped thinking you have to agree with everyone and you may find yourself saying things like, 'Actually I don't agree with that. I see it differently ...', where previously you would not have wanted to upset friends by disagreeing with them, but would secretly be angry with yourself for not expressing your true feelings, thereby creating internal stress for yourself.

- You may suddenly stop being ashamed of your rather battered old car. You may find yourself thinking that it actually doesn't matter if you don't have the latest BMW (or whatever brand you imagine you 'should' have) as you know you are respected for who you are by the people who really count, and not for what you have. You may realise that your car is a reflection of your bank balance, not your essential self, and that a funky old car is actually more individual anyway! Phew ... what a lot of stress you can release!

- You may find that you don't have the same interest in reading gossip columns in the press, or watching trivial television programmes, and this will give you more time.

- You may discover that certain tasks you undertook before suddenly seem unnecessary, so that you find a way to minimise them, or to delegate them, or simply eliminate them from your schedule. It is amazing how you can change things once you have made up your mind – and informed it of the fact! Persevere, and see how well it works.

Reviewing your agenda – 2

Another way to work with your agenda is to look at all those areas of your life at this moment that you wish you had more control over. Write them down as they come to you, no matter if they seem silly or unrealistic. Just put them down on paper – in a list, in a circle, in a pattern, inside balloons – whatever feels right; it does not matter how you do it, only that you *do* it.

Now look at each of these areas individually and ask yourself, 'Where is the "should", in this? Am I caught up in someone else's "should", or even in my own ideas of how I "should" behave or how I "should" look?' 'Shoulds' and 'oughts' are thoughts which imply someone else's control, and make us feel heavy, burdened and weighed down. If the answer is, 'Yes, I am caught up in some kind of "should" ', replace the 'I should' with 'I do not want' and see how the situation changes. Then, after the 'I do not want,' say to yourself, 'But I want …' and finish the sentence.

You may feel uncomfortable with the notion of 'I want', but just go along with it for a while, to get the flavour of what 'could be'. Or, what the possibility for your life could be if you were to give yourself what you really want rather than keeping on doing what you think you 'should' do. Even if this appears unrealistic, given all the usual constraints of ordinary life, just go with it for a while. This will give you the sense of how you might make some adjustments that could leave you less stressed, less distressed and more in control of your agenda.

Sometimes it's a question of just looking a little more deeply into the problem and finding that there is a way of doing what you want, which also manages to take care of the 'should' in a creative way.

The above exercises can reveal very important things about what is dictating your agenda.

Here are some examples to help with this exercise:

Contemplating a career move

You might have been saying to yourself (and others), 'I should stay in my rather boring job because it pays well,' but deep down you know that you feel angry and bitter at how much time you are wasting doing a job that does not really inspire you. So you then say, 'I do not want to go on with this tedious job!' Next you add, 'But I want ...' and it may be: 'But I want to work part-time, so that I can build up my graphics portfolio to help me get work I really enjoy and which uses more of my talents.' Then listen to what you have said you 'want' and take it seriously!

In this example, you could then decide that you will manage to work part-time and live on a reduced income for a while so that you can reap greater rewards later on. This way you have been honest with yourself about what you really want; the next step is working out how to make that happen. It may be that you need to accept having less money in the short-term, for the gain of doing what makes you happy and puts you more in control. At least you would now be making a conscious choice that respects and honours your true feelings about your life.

Overcoming feelings of obligation

Perhaps you are caught up in the thought: 'I should help my friend move house.' But you recognise that you feel resentful about the time you would have to spend on this when you're already feeling overloaded with all the things you need to get done in your own life. You may recognise that this is a recurring pattern: always trying to help others at your own expense. So then you eliminate the 'should', and apply the freeing technique: 'I do not want to help with the move.' After this you consider what you do want. It could be: 'But I want to be a good friend, it is important for me to be kind and supportive.' Having thought about this truth, you could tell your friend honestly that you do not have time to help with the house move, but you want to take him/her out to dinner on the evening of the move, to relieve their stress. This means you can still achieve the desire of being helpful and supportive, but in your own way – in the way that does not compromise you.

Determining your motivation

You may be saying to yourself, 'I should clean my house,' then you substitute 'should' with 'I do not want,' so you are saying, 'I do not want to clean my house.' Next you add, 'But I want ...' You may say, 'But I want a clean house.' In that case, you have two choices: clean the house yourself or find someone else to clean it. If you then decide that you cannot afford to pay anyone to do the cleaning, a creative solution to your dilemma would be to focus on the result you want, a clean environment, and so you could then decide that you 'want' to do the cleaning because you 'want a clean house'. In other words, cleaning would give you the result you 'want'.

When you change the 'I should' into 'I want' it has a different energy to it: it feels lighter and freer. However, you might have said: 'I don't want to clean the house, but I want to work on the book I am writing ... go to the cinema ... meet a friend for a drink ... paint the bedroom.' If one of those 'I wants' was judged by you to be a better use of your time, that would take you nearer to one of your life goals, then you could give up the 'I should' and make an adult decision to spend your time in the most productive way for you, thereby releasing yourself from guilt and stress.

In other words, taking control of your agenda means becoming more conscious, more aware of taking responsibility for your decisions, and believing in your right to do so!

Realising that something you thought was a 'should' part of your agenda is actually something you 'want' to do will make a huge difference to your stress levels. When you are doing what you 'want' to do, you eliminate the tension, the resentment, the lack of commitment and the potential damage to your health. You stop feeling like the underdog or the victim of things outside your control. Sometimes just affirming to yourself that you 'want' to do certain things that you *must* do can make all the difference between feeling weighed down and over-burdened, or feeling confident, effective and in control. One way to achieve this is to focus on what will be the *result* of doing what you 'should', and quite often, as in the example above, we actually 'want' the result. So if you focus your attention on the 'want', then you may find it easier to take the action that will get you to the result. If, of course, you don't see any advantage in the result of doing what you 'should' do, then what is the point of doing it?

Another way to control your agenda is to substitute the word 'should' with the word 'could'. So instead of saying to yourself 'I should do so and so,' you say 'I could do it'. This implies choice and your own autonomous control. The word 'could' means that you can if you want to, but you don't have to – there is no coercion. So you are nobody's victim, you are not manipulated and you can choose what you wish to do, to have or to be.

Prioritising your agenda

A wise elderly lady I once knew said that she always divided the demands of her life into three categories:

a.   Things which *could* be done.

b.   Things which *should* be done.

c.   Things which *must* be done.

Then she said that she tackled the 'c' category first, the 'b' category next and lastly the things in 'a'. Well, that is one way of doing it. And it is certainly a good, straightforward strategy for prioritising your tasks.

However, expanding this idea further into the arena of taking more control of your agenda, thereby controlling your stress, my suggestion is that you make three lists under the headings of the above categories, but fill in each list with the things that 'could', 'should' and 'must' be done to make you happier and more fulfilled, in other words, things for you. What you *could* do for you, what you *should* do for you and what you *must* do for you: but only you, not for anyone or anything else! And take them seriously!

This is important because it is so often the case that we do not take our own needs, and wants, seriously enough, or we relegate ourselves to the end of the list with an unspoken proviso, '… if there's any time left,' and usually there isn't! The reason for this, of course, lies in not prioritising ourselves highly enough. Do work on writing these lists, as they will be very revealing. Whether you act on them is up to you. But if you do not find yourself putting any of it into action, then, at least, ask yourself why.

Give yourself what you 'want'

I'm not suggesting that you become irresponsible and selfish, doing only what you want to do. I am suggesting that in order to feel more in control of your agenda, one of the most important steps is to make room for enough of what you 'want' to do at a deep level, as well as what you 'should' do. What you want is often related to your true self, not your everyday personality. Your personality is conditioned to 'fit in' with society, and can mask your deeper self. It's a question of balance: we are talking about having 'enough' of what you want, not everything you want. Creating some time for what you 'want' is not self-indulgent, it is life-enhancing. What I mean here is creating space in your daily or weekly agenda for the things that are connected to your core values, to your deeper self or to your creativity: these are the things that have meaning for you and bring you joy. If we spend too much of our limited time on tasks and activities that are not terribly meaningful to us in terms of our value hierarchy, we become stale and un-energised.

Even today, I think women are conditioned to put aside their own desires and focus more on the needs of others. It is difficult to get women to say what they *want*, although they will more easily talk about their needs, by which they can justify (albeit unconsciously) getting what they want. Men, however, are usually much more comfortable with doing what they want. I always encourage my women clients to develop that more masculine drive within themselves that says, 'I want!' and doesn't feel guilty about wanting, but feels important enough to be able to have what it wants. Wanting is connected to the will and the active principle; needing has more of a passive quality. Of course, they are both valid, but wants are often more fun, and fun is an essential ingredient in a successful life. Moreover, the deeper desires within us can create havoc in our lives if they are never heeded. Depression is often due to suppressing important 'wants', and disruptive behaviour in children can frequently also be traced to the same cause, precisely because some of our 'wants' are important expressions of who we truly are.

⟟ Exercise: Rethinking your agenda

Flip through your diary or possibly last year's and register your feelings as you look at what you've been doing.

- What would you like to see there more often?
- What would you like less of?
- Why are you not putting the things you want into your schedule?

Simply give yourself permission to create your agenda as you'd like it to be. Start this exercise slowly by putting into your diary just one thing each week that you want more of. It may be more 'time off from mundane tasks' – well, take it! You could code it in, if that would make you feel less guilty. For example, put: lunch M.E. or put your initials or a code name for yourself, and take yourself out to lunch. Treat this appointment in the same way as you would a lunch date with one of the most important people in your life. For you *can* be one of the most important people in your life – in fact, *you are that important person,* and you deserve to be taken out to lunch by *you!* Or, go for a walk in the park or to the movies or an art exhibition, or whatever you really want to do. Don't cancel it if something else 'important' turns up; be firm that you must honour the commitment to yourself. Treat yourself with awe and respect, and don't dare cancel! The other thing can be fitted in at another time. After all, if you had an urgent appointment with your dentist and that other 'important' event arose, you wouldn't automatically cancel the dentist, would you? Well, your 'wants' are as important as toothache! In fact, they are an ache of a kind and you must ease them; it's your responsibility.

Once you get used to this weekly treat, put two or three more special events for you into your week. You could code them S.E. (Special Event) and write: meeting with S.E. or block out certain periods that are just for you to use as you desire when the time arrives. You will actually do everything else so much more effectively when having had a little more of what you really want, for you will not be carrying so much resentment. Giving yourself time to engage with whatever you really want will probably mean you'll still get everything else done because you'll work at it with more ease and happiness.

 Case study 2: Reorganising priorities

A client of mine had a very strong-minded mother, who at ninety years of age was still running her own hairdressing business. She came from a working-class background, was very religious, had a powerful sense of the work ethic and was highly suspicious of leisure. She expected her son to think the same. For many years he worked obsessively at building up his own business until he became exhausted from overwork, which was when he came to see me. He felt guilty if he took time off to enjoy himself, but I managed to persuade him that taking holidays was not sinful, rather it re-energised him to work more productively on his return. Equally, taking time out for fun and pleasure helped not hindered his work life.

He has now reorganised his agenda to give himself more time for himself and is a happier and healthier man. His mother rings every Sunday for a chat, and if he is not there the first time she asks accusingly what he has been doing. Happily, he no longer feels guilty about looking after his own needs and wants but he has no wish to upset his mother, so he tells her he was at church, although he is usually out lunching with friends and enjoying himself. This satisfies her, for she cannot change her ways, and it stops any quarrels or tensions between them, which would be pointless at this stage of their relationship. In this respect he is actually looking after his mother as well as himself. This may appear deceitful, but you don't have to burden others with your guilty feelings about doing what you want to do. If my client had 'confessed' truthfully to his mother, it would have meant that he was still playing the child role looking to his parent for approval or permission. As adults we ultimately only have to answer to ourselves. If you know you need to change your agenda in certain ways, then the only permission you need is your own.

I am not encouraging indulgence; it is more a matter of recognising that no parent figure or fairy godmother out there is going to make sure that our lives are as we want them. We have to do it for ourselves, and believe we can!

The reason that most people don't create the lives they really want is because they don't think they can. What I am saying is: just give it a little try, start with small things and see how possible it is. When we really believe that something can happen, it does. I'm not suggesting that you can become a millionaire overnight, or a genius, or anything fantastic. I am simply saying you can dictate the content of your agenda more than you may think. The more you do this, the more you will believe you can. You will strengthen your willpower and your belief in it.

It takes a certain amount of self-discipline to action this necessary concept, and discipline may have negative associations for you with school, teachers and other authority figures. However, self-discipline, by its very nature, eliminates the need for outside authorities, so it actually frees you up. In fact, this can be one of the first steps in offloading baggage. Rid yourself of other people's authority voices in your head and replace them with just one – your own!

Offload unnecessary baggage

Often we carry on with old ways of behaving, or old images of ourselves, which are not appropriate any longer, and these may be some of the things that have to go. You may have needed certain adaptations at one time, in order to cope, but you may have outgrown them. The old coping mechanisms or beliefs and attitudes can become handicaps when they have gone past their 'use by' date.

For example, a client of mine felt that she was not connecting properly with the people around her; she said her relationships were unfulfilling and unrewarding, and that people did not react to her as she wished they would. She asked me, 'Is there something I am doing that is causing this problem – do I need to change something in my behaviour?' I suggested that she live with the question for a while and attempt to observe herself as objectively as possible. So she pondered on this; she watched herself carefully when with her friends and listened more acutely to what she was saying. She began to realise that she was not actually presenting herself to the outside world in a manner that reflected how she felt inside. She was making too many jokes and appearing to treat trivially issues that were in fact extremely important to her. She was not taking herself seriously and so others did not either.

Through the work we did together, my client discovered that she had always experienced difficulty believing in herself and in her right to have views and opinions, expecting to be ridiculed, or dismissed. She was the youngest child with four older brothers who had paid little attention to her during her childhood, except to laugh at her when she played the fool.

This became the way she gained their attention and a glimmer of admiration. Thus she got into the habit of playing the court jester, making the trivialising joke or dismissive statement first in order to protect herself from rejection. She took on the 'joker' role with school friends as well for it made her popular; but as time went by it became unfulfilling to be seen only as a clown. Once she understood more clearly how this adapted behaviour had originated she began to feel a new sense of freedom and very tentatively started to express more honestly what she really thought or felt, courageously risking dissent or dismissal from others although mostly it didn't come.

Gradually her confidence and belief in herself grew. Also her relationships felt more real and meaningful and, to her great surprise, she found people listening with respect and, in fact, taking her seriously. She did not lose her sense of humour, but stopped using it as a barrier or weapon to hold people at bay. She learnt how to honour and reveal other sides of her character as well. This demonstrates how something that works at one time in our life isn't necessarily successful forever, and may need rethinking. My client is now more relaxed and happy than ever before in her life, for she has been able to throw away a protective habit that was no longer protecting her but imprisoning her, by cutting her off from others.

Take time to consider what you have outgrown, be they attitudes or material objects. Shedding these will free you up to feel more in control.

What to offload

𝝌 Exercise: Offloading stress

Ask yourself:

- What would give me just so much relief not to have to deal with anymore?
- What or who do I wish I never had to see again?
- What would I love to get rid of in myself?

It is your life, and only you can decide what is good, or bad, for you. That includes the people you have around you. Some things should remain with us for our entire life if they are valuable to us, for whatever reason – even if others may consider them clutter or junk, or undesirable. I do not subscribe to the opinion that if you have not worn, or used, something in the past twelve months then it should be chucked out. That's much too formulaic. We are each unique and have to make the specific decisions for ourselves, honouring our own feelings. Even certain people that others consider undesirable may be in your life for a reason, and may give you valuable input, lessons or simply an experience that you need for your personal growth and development. I think the best way to judge this is at the feeling level: when we listen to our feelings they rarely lie.

If certain things are making you feel uncomfortable or unhappy, whether they are possessions past their 'use by' date which are cluttering up your life, relationships that do not fulfil you (in spite of trying hard at them), activities you no longer enjoy or traits in yourself that do not serve you positively, then you may want to consider parting company from them and no longer giving them your valuable time and energy.

Often, of course, we discover wonderful treasures in the process of clearing out our clutter.

 Case study 3: Sifting the clutter from the treasure

A client of mine had a treasured collection of letters from special people ranging over many years of her life, which she said affirmed her life and gave her pleasure to read through from time to time, especially if she felt down or depressed. She told me of the day she was looking through a box of letters which she thought were from her ex-husband, but which she discovered were actually from her to him! He had obviously kept them, and when they had separated the letters must have been mistakenly put with her things so they went with the wrong person.

But did they? She was suffering from rather low self-esteem on the day she decided to look through this box, and she thought that his letters might hold some clues about their relationship split and where she'd gone wrong. But as she read through the letters she had written to him she was shown a picture of someone rather interesting, witty and bright, and she couldn't find the evidence of her inadequacy, awfulness or badness that she felt convinced was the truth. Instead, the truth about her 'OK-ness' was in front of her. They were treasures indeed for her, although someone else might consider them clutter. So we have to become clear and strong in ourselves about what constitutes clutter and doesn't help, and what is supportive and necessary even though it may be taking up space.

If I know that certain possessions like books, clothes, or some of the objects I have inherited, make me feel good and uplift me, then no one is going to persuade me I should get rid of them. Those things are my friends, they cheer me up on a regular basis, make me smile to myself, and therefore serve a totally valuable purpose. However, if some of the things in your house, in your outer life or even in your friends make you feel upset and stressed you may need to decide to take a deep breath and say 'goodbye' to them. Don't do this in a negative state of mind: feel love for whatever you are letting go, wish it well, but affirm to yourself that you are moving on. Then feel the relief, feel the release.

To sum this up rather simplistically, a neat little yardstick to apply to your agenda is:

'If it doesn't make you happy, chuck it! If it makes you happy, keep it!'

Make space for your mind

One of the most important needs in our overfilled agendas is to find space and rest for our minds. It is far more tiring to use your mind than your body. The reason children can be so active from morning till dusk, which can be exhausting for adults, is because they do not have so much 'stuff' in their minds.

As we all know, one of today's big problems is excess of information; there is so much to absorb and so many new things coming at us every day that it is hard not to feel overwhelmed mentally. Even though much of it may be very exciting and interesting, too much of anything, no matter how good, just adds up to overload. News, views and innovation incessantly pouring out at us from various sources is extremely demanding of our mental resources. No wonder people's nervous systems are on overdrive!

Mental strain and jittery nerves result from being focused too much on the outer world: the world of sense impressions. It is fatiguing to the mind to be constantly focused outwards; the brain needs to focus inwardly as well, in a rhythmical, balanced way. We have imaginations and memory, and if we don't use them sufficiently they atrophise. Most people do not spend enough time looking inwards; reflecting on things, thinking, imagining. This is why we need to sleep regularly to switch off from the outside world. Even during the waking day we still need to rest and balance the mind. It is for this reason that meditation has been practised in India and much of the East for centuries. It gives the balance to sense-orientated impressions, putting the mind into another mode, with brainwaves often slowed down, which can be as refreshing as a night's sleep. This is one of the ancient wisdoms from which we can learn much.

⊀ Exercise: Clearing the mind

Make some special space for your mind and your nerves and give them a break from working overtime all the time! Put regular slots into your timetable for resting and nourishing your mind.

- To start with just take five or ten minutes to stare out of the window and rest your mind on the sky, trees or whatever you see.
- Close your eyes for a few minutes and imagine a white sheet of paper, which is very calming. Think of it as a kind of mind 'fast'. Let whatever you have been concentrating on slip out of your mind for a moment or two. You can't actually think about nothing (unless you are a highly developed yogi) but if you imagine a blank sheet of white paper for a few seconds, a number of times a day, it will refresh your mind.
- Put aside half an hour to listen to some soothing music; memories are often triggered by music, which can take you on an inward journey picturing places you've visited or happy times with friends.
- Take your mind on refreshing journeys in the outside world: take a walk around the block or through the park or some beautiful garden square and be nourished by the magical sights of nature.
- Bathe your mind regularly with other uplifting images like paintings, sculpture, or inspiring architecture.

Give yourself time to look inwards, and to visualise internally. Wander through your imagination and dream, as this is refreshing and balancing. In fact, it is only by dreaming, visualising, imagining, that we can create the future. A recent quote I came across emphasises this thought:

'Dreaming is not limited to the unreal. Dreaming is stretching the real beyond the limits of the present.'

One really inspiring inward-focused activity I recommend is to imagine your life as you would really like it to be. Create an inner picture of different aspects of your life, for example: where you would like to live, your ideal house, your ideal interior; then see yourself as you'd most like to be, interacting with friends and family. Imagine everything as clearly and completely as you can. Or, if you wish to change your job or career, picture yourself working in the job/career you'd like instead or picture yourself going for the interview for that job. If we do not have a vision for what we would like to create in our outer life, then it is very difficult to make it come true. But when we create a clear picture of what we are aiming for, it is amazing how much easier it becomes to achieve it. So this could be the way for you to begin spending more time on the inner dimension.

As you practise the visualisation techniques I give you throughout the book, you will begin to create your own inner landscape of wonderful and soothing places you can go to whenever the outer world feels too stressful and demanding or overwhelming.

Ⲭ Exercise: Finding a sense of peace through visualisation

When you have little time, visualise just one object or symbol that calms you: like a lighted candle, a cross, a rainbow, a gently flowing river, a tree or a white rose. By varying the inner pictures you are giving yourself a sort of inner work out, and strengthening your ability to focus your mind on whatever you decide.

Switch to the creative side of the brain

When you observe pictures or create picture images in your mind, you switch from the logical, left hemisphere of the brain into the right, creative and holistic side. This is the part of the brain that often produces creative solutions to everyday problems. It is where new thoughts and ideas can arise in the absence of the logical, linear thought processes. This is where inspiration springs from, things you had never dreamed of before. The left hemisphere of the brain tends to produce thoughts based on the past, on what is already known, whereas, when you drift and dream and visualise, you allow your mind to become free from the logical, analytical, focused world and enter the realm of possibilities, of potentiality. New ideas, inventions and all creations come from the imagination. Allow your imagination to speak to you.

Meditation

Meditation is very similar to the practice I have been advocating above although it requires greater concentration and discipline. It is a disciplining of the mind to remain focused on one thing only and not to allow other thoughts, or inner chatter, to distract the mind away from its concentration on the 'mantra' (the word/sound), the chanting, or the dance movement for a set period of time. This concentration quietens the mind, bringing it into the present moment, and it is actually a freeing of the mind from our worries, anxieties, and all the other fairly useless chatter that goes on most of the time. It is a very important antidote to our busy, frantic society and you may want to learn this practice.

There are many forms and methods for practising meditation. Some focus on concentrating the mind by giving the practitioner a word or sound to repeat inwardly, but which has no association with their everyday life. This is intended to lift them to a higher level of consciousness away from the mundane to a transcendental state. Other forms of meditation may focus on movement or chanting. All methods are aimed at taking the practitioner to an altered state of perception, to an experience that transcends our everyday stresses and worries, showing us how to become more peaceful, calm and joyful by connecting to the eternal. The method you choose will depend on your personal inclination and your goals. There are many schools of meditation (see Useful Addresses) where you could join a group for instruction and meditation practice, you can search for an individual teacher or look in your local bookstore where you are bound to find a number of instruction books.

Resting the mind

A friend of mine, who is a high-powered television producer, always takes at least twenty minutes at lunchtime to shut herself away and be quiet. Her assistants are instructed not to disturb her, just as if she were in an important meeting. Of course, she *is* in an important meeting – with herself! She lies on the floor of her office and practises some relaxation techniques and then takes herself on a guided daydream to a beautiful place in the countryside. When she re-emerges she is ready to deal with the second half of the day; she is refreshed and has realigned herself.

It is vitally important to rest the nervous system. You will have greater energy and stamina from taking regular 'mind breaks' rather than from those regular coffee breaks! Your mind needs a rest from too much stimulating sensory input.

If you think about it, what is it that actually goes to sleep when we sleep? Is it our heart or our liver or kidneys? No, all of our organs continue to work when we are asleep. It is the nervous system that sleeps, that cuts off from the world. This is absolutely essential if we are to function rationally and effectively during the day. We all know how it feels not to have enough sleep, you cannot think straight. The mind needs a rest from sense impressions, transmitted through the nervous system, and in sleep we are protected from outer sense impressions. This is really the main purpose of sleep – it's like turning the computer off.

The more help and rest we give the mind and nervous system, not just by switching off in sleep, at night, but by switching inwards from time to time during our day, the better the mind will work when we return to focus on the outside world.

⊼ Exercise: Reaffirming your right to a clear mind

Practice saying to yourself: 'Just because it's out there, it doesn't mean it has to be in here' – that is, in your mind and nervous system. Avoid cluttering up the internal you.

Einstein is reported to have said that he never attempted to remember people's telephone numbers – he maintained they were written down somewhere and he never cluttered his mind with anything unnecessary. You may think that memorising certain phone numbers *is* necessary, but the practices of a genius should not be ignored so I would advise that you simply apply the general principle in a way that is appropriate for you. Taking the advice of people who are successful is always sensible life management.

Imitate successful behaviour

Watching and learning from successful people or people you admire is a marvellous way to improve your performance in life. If someone is functioning in a stress-free manner and coping well with life's demands, then try to observe very carefully how they do it: how they structure their time, how they prioritise their tasks, how they deal with others, and so on. As children we learn everything by imitation, by copying the people around us, and I see no shame in continuing to do this throughout adult life. There will always be someone ahead of us who has cracked the code to certain of life's riddles and from whom we can learn.

> ⍟ **Exercise: Imitation is the highest form of flattery**
>
> Take time to observe someone you admire attentively. What is it they are doing that you are not? Instead of wasting energy envying someone else, use your energy to consider what it is that makes them more successful and then copy them! This is another aspect of offloading your burdens; or rather, transforming your burdens into their polar opposite. So, don't envy, but emulate!

Don't criticise yourself

However, don't put yourself down by admiring someone else *too* much. A wonderful quote sent to me by a friend recently sums this up:

'We become whole by withdrawing our projections and owning our own talents and skills.'

I think that is such a lovely twist on the usual connotation of projections, which are generally seen as being those negative, dark parts of ourselves that we do not acknowledge, but ascribe to others. The thought that what we admire in someone else could be our own hitherto unseen talents, skills or qualities is delightfully uplifting, and not usually considered. I have always believed this is what happens in hero-worship – we give away our own hero when we admire someone too much. When we adulate pop stars, film-stars or sports heroes we neglect to express the 'star' within ourselves. Carl Jung, in fact, stated many years ago, that whatever we admire in another, we possess within ourselves. For if we did not contain that particular quality or ability, he said, we would not be able to recognise it in someone else. So whatever you admire about somebody, just start to develop that potential in yourself. It's there lying dormant or just escaping your notice.

Let go of the negative self-talk. Answer it back! You don't have to take critical remarks from anybody, not even yourself! I have a voice inside that I call Carp. It carps on about this and that not being right, and I just tell it (in a most loving way, of course) to shut up! Sometimes I converse a little more intelligently with it, explaining very patiently that things are not always perfect and that I certainly am not. Moreover, I should not be expected to be perfect, for nobody is, and I personally think we should all allow each other a few frailties and inadequacies. That's how I keep this inner critic at a distance, I just don't buy everything it comes up with. We have to take responsibility for not allowing our inner critics to undermine us, so that we can get on with the task of becoming all that we were intended to be.

An inspiring saying I have pinned up in my hallway from Eleanor Roosevelt is:

'No one can make you feel inferior without your consent.'

This is exactly right. Not even you yourself – so withhold your consent!

Create clear boundaries

One other very important aspect of taking more control of our agendas and our lives is to be clear about our boundaries. It is vital to set limits and then be firm about sticking to them. This stops us feeling blown about all over the place or subject to other people's agendas. In the next chapter I address the very important need to say 'No!'

We can all find it hard to utter this word in certain circumstances, so turn over to read my suggestions about how to go about setting up firm boundaries and safe space.

Chapter 6

The positive 'No'

Unclear boundaries cause a great deal of stress, both for ourselves and other people. We are often afraid to say 'No', for fear of offending or upsetting others, but then we get pushed beyond our limits or find ourselves doing things we really didn't want to do, or we allow others to encroach on our space and time to our own detriment. How often has this happened to you? How often have you wished you'd said 'No'?

Saying 'No' is a way of protecting yourself. This little word can help you to create more of what you want in your own life, so in that sense it is one of the most useful words in your vocabulary. This is why I want to put before you the notion of the 'Positive No'. It has a different nuance. We often fear to use the word 'No', or feel upset when it is used towards us, simply because we give it a negative connotation. But if we could see 'No' as a positive utterance then we might see its creative advantages. It is positive because it makes things clear and gives us the power not to be pushed around by other people – it helps us to control our stress.

If you believe in your right to use the word, 'No' asserts your ego (your sense of self) and can be used to free you up. It is very simple. It is a way of declaring where your limits lie. We can make things extraordinarily complicated for ourselves, but this simple word is all you need. It is quite amazing where we can end up by simply failing to say 'No'. Just reflect on the undesirable things you have brought upon yourself by saying 'Yes' or 'Maybe' when you should have said 'No'.

It is important to recognise that while someone else may experience your 'No' as a negative impact, when seen from your own position it is acutely positive, and treats you with the respect and consideration you deserve. It defends your rights and sensibilities. A recent quote I came across says it well:

'When I say no to a request for my time, I am not going away from that person, I am going towards myself.'

Actually, when we put down boundaries, we are making life easier for everyone: we are providing clarity. When we do not recognise and acknowledge our limits, we often end up carrying a great deal of resentment, which is uncomfortable and gives us baggage we don't need. However, we must take responsibility when we don't say 'No', for not having marked out the boundary and thereby causing ourselves unnecessary stress. If you don't tell someone where the limits lie, you can't really blame them for not knowing! This is all about acknowledging genuine limits, not selfishness or excuses. Each one of us has limits to our energy and patience, our ability to absorb information and to the amount of time available in each day, week, month or year for particular tasks. The problem occurs when we don't state our boundaries and we often end up not only feeling angry and put-upon (sometimes upsetting others in the process as well) but also not being who we could be. If we give our time to people or things that don't really need us, or allow our energy to be leached, we have insufficient of either for our own achievements. The most successful people are very careful about how they spend their hours and how they use their energy.

Using the 'Positive No' enables you: it is not resistant or drawing you away from life. It frees you to say 'Yes' to the things that will take you forward, that will enable you to achieve your desired goals, and not get sidetracked down a cul-de-sac.

I think women have more of a problem with setting clear boundaries than men because it is a woman's nature to be more diffuse. Women can usually handle a number of tasks at once whereas men are happier dealing with one thing at a time in a linear fashion. This means that men are often more focused and single-minded in their endeavours, which makes it easier for them to say 'No' to distractions or sidetracks. And it often means that women take on far too much!

But it is not always only women who find it difficult to say 'No'. A male client of mine, who is a very enlightened business consultant and author, was having a big problem with this issue. He is constantly swamped with requests to give talks, or to meet with individuals and groups to discuss his ideas and visions, and he can't resist saying 'Yes'. He has a very generous nature and finds himself endlessly agreeing to encounters he later regrets or which he discovers have been a complete waste of time from his point of view, with people merely wanting to draw on his inspiration and energy and who offer very little in return. He has just stuck a note to himself on his telephone which reads 'Say "No!".'

A part of the problem can be that we have been brought up to believe that we must consider others first, and not be selfish; this was certainly true in the case of my client. His conditioning, coupled with a compassionate nature, meant that he genuinely wanted to be of service. But always saying 'Yes' when sometimes he should have said 'No' became undermining, as he was being drained by other people and couldn't give himself enough of what he really needed. Eventually, after we had explored this issue, and importantly, uncovered his unconscious desire to be liked by everyone, he began to see that to be selfish in the right way is actually respecting yourself and becoming more 'self-like' and peaceful.

Being true to yourself generally causes you to feel more at one with yourself. When you are being true to yourself you are also able to be more true to others. Remember the lines from *Hamlet* (Act I: Scene III):

> *'This above all: to thine own self to be true,*
> *And it must follow, as the night the day,*
> *Thou canst not then be false to any man.'*

So honour your 'self' by being clear about where you stand. Take yourself seriously – if you don't, others won't. This does not mean you have to be rude or unkind, you just have to be clear in your own mind first and then in your interactions with others. Boundaries can be time and space related. If you know you have a time limit in a meeting, for instance, state it at the outset so there is no confusion. Other people will often want to push you beyond your stated limit, but as you have already told them what time the meeting has to end you should feel no guilt in sticking to it. One of the best ways to avoid others' attempts to provoke guilt in you is to appear very surprised that they have not taken your initial statement seriously. Never justify – just stick to your message that this is the time you have to leave. A very dear, and very busy, friend of mine always arrives at my house with a huge clock which he heaves out of his bag and places somewhere extremely visible. He then tells me how long he can stay, and when the clock reaches that time he rises and leaves! Simple! I am sometimes a little dismayed that he can cut short whatever interesting topic we are focused on, but I have to say that I respect his resolve.

Establishing boundaries

To establish clear boundaries it is not always necessary to actually say 'No'. Sometimes you just have to think it. But you then have to act it in your body language. In other words, it is no good thinking 'No' and acting 'Yes'. We often give confusing signals.

Another friend tends to do this. She has very weak boundaries and I often end up having to create them for her. At the end of an evening together at my house she will very often keep saying she must go but never does! She remains sitting where she is rather than getting up and moving her body towards the door. So she is saying that she has reached a boundary but does not act on it. This can be not only confusing to others but irritating. It can be one hour or even two after the first protestations that she should leave, before she finally gets up and does so. When I am very tired I find this extremely annoying. If you make a statement that needs to be followed up by action, but you don't take the action, it leaves everyone confused as to what exactly is going on! If this happens – as it frequently can between friends or business colleagues – you have to decide that you will take the action to firm up the boundary limit. Therefore with my friend, after the second or third announcement of her imminent departure, I usually stand up and say something like, 'Shall I get your coat?' Or 'Where did you put your bag?' Or 'Yes, I am feeling very tired, I think I need to get to bed.' If she still doesn't move I open the door of the room we are in and walk slowly toward the front door. Or, I might get up and go to the bathroom, come back and remain standing, signalling that the evening is over.

What I am actually signalling is that now I am taking control of putting down the boundary. I left it to her for quite a long time, out of consideration and politeness, but now I've reached my limit. I'm saying that this particular evening is ending and I don't feel guilty about it. We each have a right to be able to control our space and time in this way. Sometimes both parties may be vacillating with neither being clear about what they want to do.

When this happens you can feel the energy seeping away because each person is denying their inner drive to go for what they really want and therefore their energy is being suppressed; it feels very uninspiring.

Say 'No' with a 'Yes' voice

If you want to say 'No', but think you should be saying 'Yes', it is often because you think or feel that 'No' is somehow rude or offensive. The way round this one is to say 'No' with a 'Yes' voice! Practise this by saying 'Yes' to yourself when you're alone, then say 'No' in exactly the same way. When we say 'Yes' we use a different and usually more positive tone. The tone of your voice has the most important impact. It has been discovered in research studies that our tone conveys the message much more powerfully than our words.

⍓ Exercise: Changing your intonation

Practice saying 'No' with uplift at the end, as you would with 'Yes'. Usually 'No' is said in a very final tone, with a forceful and abrupt ending. Try saying it with a slightly lingering ending. Then combine the lingering sound with the uplifting or positive tone. This can never sound offensive, or aggressive but it is still 'No'! In fact, it is the 'Positive No'. The important point is that you should not make people feel they are being rejected or given the brush-off. It is not against them – it is *for* you.

Saying 'No' with a 'Yes' voice is a way of protecting yourself from the stress of being pushed into doing things you don't really want to do, or which are wasting your time and energy and not helping you to achieve your objectives. It gives you the key to stepping out of the victim role, side-lining the stress, and taking control and responsibility for creating your life the way you want it to be.

Visualising boundaries

Other ways of putting your boundaries in place can be achieved symbolically or imaginatively through visualisation. One client of mine visualised putting on her imaginary blue cloak when she went to visit her extremely demanding elderly aunt; this made her feel protected from the pathetic but aggressive comments intended to make her feel guilty for not giving more of her time. She was a very sensitive young woman, who genuinely felt a great deal of compassion for her aunt, but who simply could not give her anymore time as she was a single parent with a small child to look after as well as having a demanding job. So putting her boundary in place meant that she could give a certain amount of care and affection, but would not be sucked into colluding with the older woman's complaints, which would have meant visiting for longer and neglecting essential aspects of her own life.

Another client recently visualised a bubble around herself, which kept others at a distance and protected her from their negative 'vibes'. She felt safe when she was inside her bubble. She is a social worker and often receives abuse from people she is trying to help or from those from whom she is trying to protect others. She really needs her bubble!

A recent divorcee imagined a Perspex shield protecting her heart and solar plexus from too much emotional contamination or emotional blackmail. And a male client said he could visualise a giant sieve around himself, which allowed the finer particles through but kept out the gross, unrefined stuff coming at him from others, or from the general environment. This made him feel more in control, and more peaceful about his life situation.

A woman who felt extremely vulnerable visualised a concrete wall between herself and the world, but on her side she created a gentle stream flowing around the bottom of the wall and a beautiful garden. In the wall itself she had narrow slits like in fortress castles, which she could see through, but at which she also had powerful guns positioned in case she should need to blast anyone! A little extreme, but that was what gave her the strength to engage with the world. She knew she could always withdraw mentally behind her wall, where she felt safe and protected from anyone that upset her, or made her feel threatened.

⍟ Exercise: Visualise your boundaries

If you are feeling over-run by someone, or intruded upon, visualise a protective barrier between yourself and the other person. This is your secret way of saying 'No'. Some people have used a piece of clothing, a cloak for example, which they visualise putting around their body to keep the other person out.

Physical boundaries

Sometimes an actual physical item can be used to provide a secret, but tangible, protective barrier in certain circumstances. A colleague of mine had a very difficult relationship with her elderly mother. She was continually hurt by her mother's criticisms and barbed remarks. She loved her mother, and really didn't want to stop seeing her, but decided she had to do something to protect herself. So she took to wearing a wide belt with a huge silver buckle whenever she visited. She visualized to herself that the buckle was a protective shield, and that the hurtful things her mother said just bounced off it, like bullets ricocheting off a tin can. This really helped her not to react inwardly quite so intensely, as she used her buckle to help her block the painful words from penetrating.

✝ Exercise: Erecting physical boundaries

If you are not good at visualising, try holding some everyday object in front of the solar plexus region (in front of your stomach, where emotion is felt most acutely) if you have to be in situations which make you nervous or stressed in some way, for example, if you have to attend an important interview or a meeting with your boss. What I often recommend to my clients is that they carry a newspaper, a briefcase, a cardboard file or, if appropriate, a handbag or even gloves, and that they then hold the item across their solar plexus region and imagine it is a protective barrier that nothing can penetrate; a sort of shield that they are safe behind. This can give you confidence as it makes you feel protected, but is not obvious to others. Alternatively, you can simply clasp your hands together – not too tightly – or just put one on top of the other, and hold them in front of your stomach, imagining they are your shield that nothing unpleasant can penetrate, giving you the protection you need.

Establishing 'safe space'

It is vital for controlling our stress levels, as well as for our general well-being, that we have not just time but also space for ourselves, and to feel that we can control our space. You may allow others in when you decide, but the point is that you feel you have the control and the right to say 'No, not now'. If you are feeling encroached upon, and are having difficulty achieving this in an aspect of your outer life, it can also be achieved through visualisation. You can create the perfect space for yourself in your imagination, and go there whenever you have some time alone. This can be wonderfully affirming of your inner life and your own autonomy; in other words, of your right to withdraw from the outside world whenever you choose, into a beautiful interior world. As I have already said, I consider it most important that we recognize the reality of our inner world and feel comfortable and peaceful within ourselves. The more you become the creator of beautiful thoughts and images inside yourself the less you will feel a stranger there.

It is also important to create some kind of sanctuary in the outer world as well if you possibly can, a space that belongs to you and no one else. Somewhere you can go to be alone and in peace, or in any state you want at that moment. You may want to play a particular kind of music or read or watch a DVD or just sleep. If you live alone it will not be too difficult to organise this, but if you have a family or live with a partner or friend, try to have one place that feels like your own 'safe space' or your own stress-free zone.

 Case study 4: Establishing personal space

A client of mine had moved into his girlfriend's house after separating from his wife, and was feeling somewhat destabilised and not too comfortable. He wondered why he was not feeling happier. We did a visualisation exercise and he asked himself where exactly in his mind, body or emotions he was experiencing the discomfort. Eventually it dawned on him that he had no sense of really belonging in the new house. I asked him what might give him that feeling of belonging, and he realised that he greatly missed his desk from his former home: it had felt like 'his inviolate territory'. This realisation was very important to my client and he went out the next day and bought himself a desk! It was the beginning of really feeling 'at home' in his girlfriend's house: the desk was 'his space'. As time went by he also took some control of other aspects of the space in which he now lived, how it was ordered and decorated, and they became true partners. But he needed his desk to give him his sense of selfhood. It was almost symbolic: a little like a child when away from home needing to

take a special toy which connects them to a safe space at home
or a comfort blanket which makes them feel safe.

⊼ Exercise: Building your safe space

Find an area and organise your own safe space. It can be your
own room (a spare bedroom or study is ideal), but even a part of
a room reserved only for your possessions, or a desk that
belongs to you and which no one is allowed to invade without
your invitation, would give you that necessary personal safe
space.

Your own personal stress-free zone could also be a space of
time, so that, for instance, you take half an hour, or an hour, when
you regularly withdraw into your bedroom to meditate, visualise,
or practise your relaxation routine: and this is respected as
inviolate by the rest of your household. You can establish that you
are not allowed to be disturbed, except in an emergency, for this
is your 'sacred' space. Equally, you could instigate this kind of
'time space' in your daily routine at your office, as does my friend
the television producer whom I mentioned in Chapter 5, who
takes time in the middle of the day to be alone, firmly believing in
her right to give herself this space of time.

If you do not have a private office, put space for you into your
timetable each week by going to sit quietly at lunchtime in a
church, or even in a park or garden square. Or, possibly just take
time regularly to go out for lunch alone so that you can go into
your own interior space. Even if you are reading during that time,
you are still connecting with your inner self of thoughts and
feelings, and this takes you to another place. When you return
you will feel refreshed simply because of the change of focus.

You have the right to set limits and establish boundaries and to
protect them from being trampled down by others. Feeling that

you have more control over your space and time will release you from a great amount of inner stress and should give you a feeling of greater ease generally. But the only way you achieve this is by using the 'Positive No' – in all its manifestations.

Chapter 7

Stress at work

Each year millions of working days are lost through illness, much of it resulting from stress in the workplace. The UK Health and Safety Executive define work-related stress as: 'a harmful reaction people have to undue pressures and demand placed on them at work.' The HSE recognises stress as 'the biggest single cause of work-related illness.' However, the latest estimates from the Labour Force Survey show the total number of cases of work-related stress in 2010/11 was significantly lower than the number in 2001/2. This indicates that stress at work is nowadays being taken more seriously than in previous decades, and many companies and organisations are taking measures to address the causes of stress, as well as putting relevant support structures in place. Nevertheless, the problem of stress has not completely vanished from the workplace, and in this chapter we shall look at the many contributing factors that create stress at work together with practical suggestions for its better management.

A too heavy workload

A heavy workload seems to be one of the principal causes of stress, as more and more pressures are heaped upon individuals in a world that wants everything done faster, and where competition is becoming fiercer all the time. The need for people to perform to their maximum capacity has never been greater. Again, we are back to the problem of 'overload' that we discussed in Chapter 5. And, as we established there, everyone has a limit. You can push yourself – or be pushed – to extremes for a short time, but not as a way of life and certainly not every day of your working life.

There are, of course, times when an extreme workload is unavoidable in order to complete a project on time or due to absenteeism among colleagues, but this should not be your 'norm'. If you feel unfairly overloaded it is important to make this clear to your boss or your line manager. It may well be that your boss, or whoever is supervising, does not realise the strain you are under because you have valiantly tried to cope without complaint. But you cannot cope indefinitely with too much work to fit into reasonable working hours. You must discuss your situation with your immediate superior. However, before you request a meeting, it is essential that you have thought about possible solutions.

Just complaining won't usually get results; you need to have some suggestions as to how to solve the problem. These may include delegating to a colleague, hiring additional temporary staff to help with the emergency or expanding the work team by taking on extra permanent staff. At the same time try to take into consideration the fact that your manager may also be under considerable pressure from above to hit certain targets, or might be new to that job and feeling insecure or unsure about how to manage their team initially. It has been noted in many studies that middle managers often suffer the most work-related stress due to being pressurised from two directions – from the more senior levels above, and from those below their level, who are under their management. But if you are feeling overloaded too much of the time, you must take action to address the situation so that your health does not suffer. Do not struggle on until you simply collapse with exhaustion and burnout.

Unclear instructions or insufficient information

Feeling unclear about what is needed or expected of you in a task can cause considerable stress. Some managers can be very vague in imparting information or just do not take the time and trouble to explain themselves clearly. It has been found in research studies that a team with clear goals and procedures works faster and has less absenteeism than those who are not clearly managed. People are often reluctant to say they don't understand an instruction or procedure for fear of looking stupid or unintelligent. But it is important to ask for clarification if you have not sufficiently understood a communication. Poor communication leads to many problems and causes much distress, both at work and in people's personal lives. Never be afraid to ask questions. So long as they are relevant questions, your desire for clarity will usually be seen as a desire to do a job properly and well. If you work in a team, it could help if you suggest the idea of regular meetings with all team members being present to encourage better and clearer communication, and this could also reveal that other members of the team are having similar difficulties and that you are not alone.

New managers often want to change certain practices and procedures, which can produce resistance from colleagues who are used to working in a particular way and don't want to change. It is important to explain the reasons for the changes, rather than to impose them without explanation, in order to ensure you get 'buy-in' from your team. Unless everybody understands the changes, and why they are necessary, the efficiency of the team or department will be adversely affected.

It is important to understand that people cannot work well if they do not fully understand what is required of them. If you are a manager, one way to ensure improved communication within your team could be to develop a practice of weekly meetings, where each person has a chance to air their problems and to discuss any improvements they feel could make a difference. Listening is as important for good communication as is giving clear instructions. Good two-way communication is vital for creating a strong culture of trust and respect, and clarity of goals and objectives (as well as of procedures) will lead to greater cooperation within a team. Again, if this is your particular stress-inducing problem, do not feel you have to keep working in the dark. If you do not get a satisfactory response from your immediate boss after you have tactfully attempted to explain how the lack of clarity or unclear communication is impacting on you and possibly the whole team, try going to a higher level; or if you work in a large organisation you should talk to Human Resources about the problem. But getting the whole team together in regular meetings seems to help significantly, and is being put into practice by many large and successful organisations as a stress-busting strategy.

Boundaries in the workplace

Boundaries are just as important in a work context as in your personal life and you need to feel able to control them. Lack of control over our space and boundaries is another stress-producing factor at work, although it is not always recognised. We all need a certain amount of space around us to feel comfortable. Psychological research has found that there are specific physical distances at which we need to keep other people, depending on our relationship with them. When we cannot maintain these distances, or have no control over them, we become uncomfortable and tense. There is a lot of talk nowadays about our 'comfort zones' as we have become more aware of this very real need to be in a comfortable space in order to function at an optimum level. If you are being overcrowded by other people at work, as much as on a train or bus, or in a crowded shopping mall, you experience distress. In overcrowded environments animals become aggressive or fearful, and due to our fundamental need to control our own space we have the same kinds of instinctive reactions. So do not think that it is pretentious or neurotic to demand sufficient space for yourself – it is normal and necessary for your well-being.

Research studies have identified four different types of space that we need to maintain in our interactions with other people depending on our relationship with them.

Intimate space

This is between 1 and 6 inches (2.5–15cm) away from us, and usually only lovers or close family are allowed into this space. Any invasion of intimate space by someone with whom we are not close causes great distress and even physical disorders if it is prolonged and we have no control over the other person. When there is nothing we can do to alter the situation, such as in a crowded train or in a queue at an airport, we tend to depersonalise it: we look through people as if they were not there, treating them as impersonal objects, or we use aggressive behaviour to hold our space and force others to retreat. If your boss or a work colleague comes too close and invades your intimate space, making you feel uncomfortable, you would be within your rights to ask them to move away a little.

Personal space

This is between 6 and 18 inches (15–46 cm) away from us, and is the comfort zone for those we trust and with whom we are close emotionally, but are not intimate. When this space is invaded by anyone outside those categories, they are transgressing our boundaries. We become tense and stiff, trying to hold them off with our body posture. Extroverted personalities can usually tolerate more intrusion of their intimate and personal space than introverts. It has also been noted that different cultures have different space needs. Cultures that could be called tribal, as well as predominantly matriarchal, family-orientated societies, such as the 'Latino' cultures, seem to be more comfortable with less personal space than the Western, more independently-minded cultures.

Social space

This is the distance between 18 inches and 4 feet (46–122cm) away from us and is the norm for more impersonal interactions like interviews, business transactions and meetings, and for formal social occasions with people who are not close friends or family. This is the ideal space requirement for our interactions at work.

Public space

This is between 4 and 12 feet (122–366cm) away from us, which is the sort of space that would feel comfortable if we were giving a lecture or presentation, for discussions and for teaching a class.

Understanding your spatial needs will help you to organise your working environment to your maximum comfort. In some offices desks are facing each other, which will mean you have someone talking and breathing directly into your personal space – even if there are computer screens separating you.

𝑋 Exercise: Creating a comfortable work environment

- Try to create a barrier between yourself and other colleagues by a strategic arrangement of plants, by placing a small bookcase at the edge of your desk or workstation, or using acoustic screens (see Useful Addresses) which are also excellent for muffling or absorbing other people's sounds. Another way of protecting your own space would be the strategic placement of cabinets and floor-standing shelves, or large floor-standing plants, if the configuration of the room and the management allows.

- Try to ensure that other people's belongings do not intrude into your workspace. If this happens frequently try to create a physical barrier with plants or books to mark the boundary line.

- Untidiness and clutter can also make you feel overcrowded and uncomfortable, so try to keep a certain amount of order and tidiness around your workspace, utilising stacking storage boxes or box files to contain clutter and paperwork. Space that looks ordered is usually more restful, so give attention to your visual environment.

- Try to make your working environment beautiful as well as functional. It's important to personalise your working space as much as you can, to bring in to your working day reminders of what is truly meaningful to you. Pin up photographs and pictures of your favourite places, or poems or sayings that uplift you, or place shells or attractive stones you've collected on, or beside, your desk to bring back memories of happy holidays; anything that reminds you of a calmer dimension will help to buffer you against unavoidable pressures and demands.

Other people's stress!

It is so easy to 'catch' other people's stress and tension. Learn to recognise when this is happening to you and instantly create an imaginary barrier between you and the other person.

⅄ Exercise: Dodging extraneous stress

If you fear absorbing stress from someone, imagine a wall between you that is high enough to protect your body, but where you can still see over the top to talk. Visualise the other person's stress just bouncing off that wall back towards them. Or imagine their stress floating up over your head and away into the ether. Practice refusing inwardly to take on other people's stress reactions: just affirm to yourself that the problem belongs to them and not to you.

It is possible to stay calm and relaxed even when those around you are worked up. Affirm to yourself that this is the case, and practice regularly the relaxation techniques outlined in Chapter 9 so that you can slip easily into the Relaxation Response when you most need it.

Constant interruptions

It can be very difficult to get through the work you have in front of you if you have constant interruptions. Interruptions interfere with a train of thought you may be having, or a particular rhythm you've got into, and so you need to use certain techniques to avoid or dismiss interrupting invaders – be it the telephone, another person or even your children, if you work from home. Listed below are a few helpful techniques you might like to try when you do not want to be interrupted:

- **Avoid eye contact:** Don't look up from whatever you're working on and simply state firmly that you cannot stop as you have a deadline to meet. If it is the telephone that has disturbed you just be firm and say you can't talk now, ask them to call back later and then say 'goodbye'. Never justify yourself, instead just state that you can't talk now.

- **Silence is golden:** If the intruder continues to demand your attention simply resist adding anything unnecessary to the conversation and again, keep eye contact to a minimum.

When the other person finishes speaking, remain silent. Do not allow yourself to be drawn into small talk.

- **Broken record:** Use the 'broken record technique'. This consists of repeating over and over again your main statement that you cannot stop right now. You just say, for example: 'I can't stop working now; I must get on with this report. I'll get back to you later', as many times as necessary for the message to sink in. It is very effective.

- **Move away:** If you have your own separate office and you want someone to leave, just get up out of your chair and begin to walk towards the door, using body language to indicate that the meeting is over, whilst making a polite but firm statement like: 'Thank you for looking in, now I must get back to work.' Or, 'I must get on with things now; can you get back to me later?' Either way, make it very clear that this is the end of the interaction.

- **Put up a sign:** You can, of course, put a sign on your door saying 'Do Not Disturb'. This can be effective if you work from home with family around you, as long as your family does not see it as rejection, but simply as a temporary signal. Train your colleagues or members of your family to respect that sign and to leave you alone (unless there is a true emergency) when you are especially busy.

- **Closing a meeting:** If you wish to bring a meeting to a close and reclaim your space, you can use similar tactics to those above. Get up out of your chair, and say something like, 'Well, it has been very interesting to meet you, and I hope we can be in touch again soon. Thank you for coming to see me.' If the other person does not respond by standing up also, and maybe tries to continue the conversation, you should walk slowly towards the door, repeating the message in slightly different words, and then stand silently, waiting near the door. This should have the desired effect. Of course, you can actually say, 'I must stop now, as I have another meeting in five minutes,' or something along these lines. But if someone refuses to take their cue and tries to keep you engaged in conversation, don't feed it. In other words, after they have spoken, don't add anything apart from perhaps a smile and a nod of your head. Just hold your ground and refuse to be sidetracked. If that doesn't work you could try the 'broken record technique', and simply repeat again and again your last statement. So you would say, 'I must stop now, I have another meeting in five minutes,' as many times as necessary. Whether you genuinely have another meeting or not doesn't matter, what does matter is that you have the right to control your time and space and put down boundaries.

Bullying and intimidation

Feeling intimidated or being bullied is often invisible and difficult to prove. Nevertheless, it can ruin someone's life. Employers are required by law to protect the health and safety of all their employees and failure to put in place appropriate measures to prevent or deal with bullying could be unlawful. Bullying must never be tolerated, and should be reported to your senior manager, supervisor, human resources department or your trade union representative. As we all know, bullies are cowards and will often resort to underhand tactics that are not easily observable, like sending emails or texts, or ganging up with other bullies to intimidate or torment. If this happens to you, keep any evidence from emails or texts or other communications and try to get a colleague you trust to be a witness to the obnoxious behaviour so that you have proof at a tribunal hearing, or if you wish to bring a legal action against your employer for not protecting you against abuse.

People sometimes use their position of seniority to intimidate those below them; or certain groups will target someone of a different ethnic group, a different gender or age, or with different religious beliefs. Never retaliate with similar behaviour as this takes you down to the level of the perpetrator. If possible, stand up to the other person with dignity, preferably when others are present, and state that their behaviour is unacceptable. You need to demonstrate that you are strong and will simply not put up with bad treatment from anyone. Managers can feel intimidated by excessive pressure to achieve ever more difficult targets in today's increasingly competitive world, and the stress they are experiencing often gets passed to others in the form of bullying. This is not good management and when it happens it indicates that someone is out of control. Often the reasons behind the bullying need addressing.

It is sometimes difficult to admit that you are a victim of bullying, but it must be addressed before it affects your health. If you cannot bring yourself to talk about bullying to anyone in the workplace you could seek out a counsellor, or talk to your parish priest or vicar, or a family member you trust. You need to get support from others as it can feel very lonely being the target of unpleasant behaviour, so do confide in the people close to you, and ask for moral support. However, if bullying or intimidation is operating within an organisation, it is imperative that it is reported to the appropriate authorities, which could include the police if physical abuse has taken place.

Symptoms of too much stress

You may recognise that you are not living as healthily as you'd like due to carrying too much stress. Some of the symptoms of stress overload are:

- Drinking more alcohol than usual
- Sleeplessness – difficulty getting to sleep at night or waking in the early hours
- Feeling more emotional than usual
- Non-specific hostility: feeling angry most of the time
- Feeling threatened by life's demands and by other people
- Increased irritability
- Humourlessness
- Eating too much, or too little
- Increased dependence on caffeine, tobacco or other mood-altering substances
- Digestive disorders
- Frequent minor ailments, like coughs, colds and flu, indicating that your resistance is low
- Excessive sweating
- Impaired memory
- Palpitations – racing heartbeat
- Difficulty making decisions
- Feeling indispensable, thinking about work all the time – never able to switch off
- Inability to relax
- Feeling the joy has gone out of life
- Always feeling rushed; always in a hurry
- Resistance to change

If you are experiencing many of the above symptoms on a regular basis they are warning signals that you are carrying too much stress. You need to reassess how you are living and which aspects of your work or your home life must be addressed and changed for the better.

Stress-inducing environmental problems

Poor lighting, fluorescent lighting or insufficient daylight

Avoid fluorescent lighting if you possibly can, or buy full-spectrum bulbs. Fluorescent lights have been found to have a very negative effect on some employees, causing headaches, skin blemishes (such lights are thought to destroy vitamin A in the skin) and in some cases they have been found to induce epileptic fitting as the older type of lights emit imperceptible flashes (although this problem is said to have been erased in the newer strip lighting). Depression has also been linked to this type of lighting. Full-spectrum bulbs contain the complete light-ray spectrum (including the ultraviolet rays that are missing in regular fluorescent tubes) which is much healthier to work under. (See Useful Addresses for where to purchase full-spectrum bulbs.)

Make sure that you have good lighting focused on your workstation so that you avoid eye strain. If overhead lighting is poor, buy yourself (or ask your employer to buy) an anglepoise lamp that can be pointed directly at whatever you need to be reading or working on. Use opaque shades to reduce glare, and point the light bulb away from your sight line.

Natural light is vital to us as it regulates the levels of the hormone melatonin, which has powerful effects on sleep, mood and the reproductive cycle. Insufficient natural light can upset these rhythms, and for some people a lack of daylight can be a serious problem in the long, dull winter months, leading to a condition known as SAD (seasonal affective disorder), which is now recognised among medical practitioners. The symptoms of SAD include depression, sleeplessness, poor concentration and carbohydrate craving. For more information on SAD contact the SAD Association (see Useful Addresses). A daily supplement of vitamin D can help relieve symptoms during the winter, as well as hiring or purchasing a daylight-simulating Light Box, which can be researched online or through the SAD Association. If there is little natural daylight in your workplace try to get out into some natural light as often as possible during lunch breaks, and during your weekends, especially when the sun is shining.

Lack of air flow, poor ventilation, air quality too hot, too dry or too cold

Research indicates that poor air quality aggravates sinus problems, allergies, headaches and respiratory problems. It can also make us feel tired and lethargic and affect concentration. Negative ion generators, also known as ionisers, can help to keep the air fresh and clear by charging it with a continuous output of healthy negative ions. The negative ions attach to particles such as dust, smoke, bacteria, pollen and other allergens and then seek out the nearest surface like a shelf or a wall, or drop down onto the floor when they become too heavy. They can then be cleaned or vacuumed from the surfaces. Negative ions are thought to be natural mood enhancers because they increase the oxygen-carrying capacity of the blood, thereby increasing the amount of oxygen reaching the brain. Positive ions, which cause poor air quality, build up in the atmosphere as a result of central heating, air conditioning, overcrowding, general pollution and low barometric pressure. Positive ions also collect around TV sets and personal computers.

You may have noticed how alive and energised you feel when near the sea. This is because negative ions are most plentiful around fast-running water and it could also be the reason why many people feel more refreshed after taking a shower than after a bath. Sea air is charged with tens of thousands of negative ions, which purify and oxygenate the air, whereas office buildings have been found to contain, at most, hundreds of negative ions, and frequently only dozens, or occasionally zero.

You can keep the air around you fresh and healthy by putting a small negative air ioniser beside your desk or workspace. In a large open-plan office, a number of ionisers placed around the room would be helpful (see Useful Addresses for how to purchase ionisers). Open windows as often as possible, even if air conditioning is operating, or traffic noise will impinge for a while. There really is nothing to beat the flow of fresh air. Keeping your workspace well-ventilated will also help to remove chemical residues from synthetic cleaning products, as well as other pollutants like dust, ozone, carbon dioxide and unappealing smells. Ventilation is especially important if there are chemical vapours in the atmosphere. Try to keep photocopiers and fax machines in a separate room, or screen them off to minimise their noise and chemical pollution.

If you have air conditioning operating keep the temperature at about 19–23°C (66–73°F) and try to maintain a comfortable level of humidity. Central heating can also cause the atmosphere to dry out and to counteract this either purchase a humidifier or place bowls of water above the radiators or around your workspace to increase humidity. This is important, as you may become dehydrated if there is insufficient moisture in the atmosphere. Keep some bottled water at your desk or workstation and drink it frequently to avoid dehydration, which can lead to drowsiness and lethargy. Also reduce coffee consumption, as coffee is dehydrating. Plants and bowls of flowers will also contribute to the humidity, as well as breathing out essential oxygen into the environment; the more plants around you the better the air quality. Research carried out in the 1980s by NASA, investigating how to keep the air fresh inside space capsules, found certain plants to be particularly good as air fresheners. These are: poinsettia, azalea, chrysanthemum, orchid, spider plant, English ivy, gerbera, lady palm and peace lily.

Stress on your body due to static postures

No matter how perfectly you position your body at your desk or workstation, it is not natural for the human body to be kept in a static posture for any length of time. Our bodies function best when they are kept moving. Take regular breaks from sitting; get up and walk around at least once every hour, and stretch your body regularly. (See Chapter 9 for stretches and movements you can practise at work.)

After two hours of continuous keyboard work mistakes become more frequent, so taking short 5–10 minute breaks will reduce your errors as well as taking the physical strain off your body. Breaks also give your mind a rest and give you a change of perspective; taking time to stand back is never time wasted because it can clear away a lot of tension and stress.

Static posture and its undesirable side effects are not only occupational hazards for people sitting at computer screens, but also for musicians, train and bus drivers, long-distance lorry drivers, pilots, people working in call centres or at check-out counters. Even guardsmen on duty outside the royal palaces are allowed to rock unobtrusively backwards and forwards from heel-to-toe to introduce a little movement into their static working day. This stimulates their blood circulation just enough to ensure they do not pass out! Movement, good posture, breathing correctly and stretching out contracted and tense muscles, will help to keep the body relaxed and de-stressed during the working day.

⅄ Exercise: Get the blood flowing

- Stretch your eye muscles by regularly focusing into the distance or out of the window, or close your eyes and circle

> them round in both directions, then look up to the ceiling and down to the floor without tilting your head, keeping your eyes closed, and then move your eyes from side to side to stretch the muscles and give them a break from a static focus.
> - Take breaks to walk around, stretch and yawn, perhaps go outside and breathe in some fresh air.
> - Jog on the spot to deepen your breathing and to stimulate your circulation.
> - Vary your tasks during the day so that you get a balance between sitting and being more active.

Working from home

Many of the problems already covered in this chapter apply equally to someone working at home. However, there are specific stresses involved in working from home. There are also, of course, advantages to this situation. One major advantage is that you are the master of your environment and you have the opportunity to create an atmosphere that is positive, supportive and creative and which enhances your productivity. You are free to personalise your space in a way that is satisfying to your individual personality. Set against this positive aspect, however, there are certain stresses that are unique to the home work situation and these are outlined below.

Isolation

As the poet John Donne famously wrote: 'No man is an island, entire of itself.' We need each other, and we function best when we can share our thoughts and ideas. However, isolation can be one of the major problems when working from home. When we are alone for long periods it is easy to lose perspective; the main problem often being that we become too critical of ourselves, with every little mistake getting blown up out of all proportion. This can lead to depression and low self-esteem; the lack of positive feedback – or any feedback – from colleagues can become eroding. So take this aspect of working on your own into account, and allow yourself some breaks from the solitary confinement. Have occasional interludes in your day when you pick up the phone and chat to a friend or colleague; this is not escapism or indulgence. Just talking to someone can energise you after many hours working silently alone and will also help you to breathe more fully. When sitting alone staring at a computer screen our breathing often becomes shallow, providing the body and brain with insufficient oxygen. There is also the tendency to hold one's breath when concentrating, but talking, and even better, laughing, deepens our breathing.

𝍐 Exercise: The importance of the spoken word

- Try singing out loud if you've been alone for many hours, just to deepen your breathing. It doesn't matter how out of tune you might be!

- Talk to people over the phone sometimes instead of sending emails. Having occasional chats with real people can help add some stimulation to your day as well as possibly giving you a different take on certain issues. The input received from others is not to be undervalued and can prevent you from becoming too introspective or taking things too seriously – especially yourself.

- Arrange regular lunch meetings with a friend or colleagues several times a month so that you have to get out and about and interact with the outside world from time to time.

- Create a social life outside of working hours when there is no social interaction during the day. Even if you enjoy your own company, it is not healthy to be too much alone. Whilst a definite up-side of being cut-off from others is that you are spared their moodiness, criticisms, bad temper or irritating habits, it is important to feel that you are still 'in the swim of things'.

Lack of energy due to lack of input from others

You may experience a lack of energy when working alone for many hours. If so, try out some of the exercises below. Some people can work with the radio or television on in the background, but this is actually very tiring for the mind, as it is fragmented by trying to listen to the media input and also concentrate on the work in hand, and it tends to overwork your nervous system. You can make up for any breaks you take by working a little later in the evening when others would be on their commute.

⫟ Exercise: Energising your working day

- Play some gentle unobtrusive music in the background. Orchestral music is best without any singing as the words of songs tend to be distracting.
- Take occasional breaks to listen to the news or watch a favourite TV programme, which is another positive aspect of working at home – so long as you can trust yourself to be disciplined about returning to work once the programme is over!
- For an extra energy boost simply go out for a short walk to the local shops, the library or just to experience some contact with your fellow human beings.

Set your own schedule

One of the great advantages of working from home is that you do not have to adhere to anyone else's schedule. Creating breaks in your schedule at whichever part of the day fits your personality can offer an important rhythm to your day as well as providing a vital energy boost by getting into a different atmosphere.

𝕏 Exercise: Are you a lark or an owl?

Set your own timetable to suit your energy cycles. You may consider yourself to be 'an owl' rather than 'a lark', in which case you might choose to start work later in the day, have a break later than most for lunch, and then continue working into the evening. If you are 'a lark' then you can start your day early and finish earlier than most office workers, leaving you with leisure time when others are at work, giving you the possibility of visiting museums, parks, art galleries or shops when there are no crowds.

Increased number of tasks

The independence gained from working alone can turn into the stress of having to do absolutely everything yourself, unless you are lucky enough to have a partner at home during the day who is prepared to take on many of the maintenance tasks. If you are alone at home you have to answer the telephone every time it rings, respond to the doorbell, put the dog out, make your own cups of tea and coffee and your own lunch, having remembered not to run out of milk or sugar and everything else you might need like paper, pens, envelopes, Jiffy bags, stamps, light bulbs, Sellotape, paper clips, ink cartridges and so on just to keep your day running along smoothly. The spread of tasks increases, and the roles you have to play increase.

Take all of this into account as you pace yourself during the working week. You will have to decide on the best sort of timetable for producing the results you need, at the same time as allowing for all the extra tasks you will have to undertake that are usually provided by others in an office setting. One of your gains, of course, is that you are saved many frustrations and much unproductive time by not having to commute to and from your place of work.

Undefined boundaries

To minimise frustrations at home, the division between workspace and home space needs to be clearly defined. Ideally you need a separate room for your work, but if this is not possible then at least have clear divisions within the living space between work equipment and the things that belong to your home life. Take time and trouble to create a supportive and artistic environment for yourself that will enhance your work.

⍓ Exercise: Reinvigorating your home work environment

- If you work on the kitchen or dining-room table, purchase some appropriate files, multi-layered trays or wicker baskets, to store away your work things at the end of the day. Papers, pens, books, highlighters and so on scattered about, or randomly balanced in wobbly, untidy piles all around the house will cause you stress, anxiety and muddled thinking. If papers and work equipment are neatly contained you will feel more ordered and organised and will be able to find everything you need to slip seamlessly into work the next day. Wallet-type files are very useful and can be clearly marked on the outside so that the contents are easily identifiable. Be imaginative about the storage items you choose, so that they look attractive and artistic, not merely utilitarian.
- Try to make your environment stimulating and inspiring; add flowers or plants.

> • Burn energising incense or essential oils like sandalwood, rosemary, patchouli or bergamot as uplifting scents can lift your energy levels. Have bowls of positive smelling pot-pourri, lavender or rose petal sachets, around your work area. Indulge your senses to uplift your spirits.

If you use certain rooms during the day for working or having meetings, be clear about when they revert back to being available for family or social use. Make sure members of your family, or people you share with, are also clear about these divisions, and preferably have had some say in the way they have been arranged. This ensures their goodwill, which is important in supporting you in your working endeavours. Clear time divisions are also important. Set definite times for beginning and finishing the working day and be disciplined about sticking to them.

Self-discipline

Self-discipline is an issue when working from home. One has to be firm with oneself about getting started and about staying put when domestic or social interruptions threaten to distract you from the task in hand. Just say to yourself: 'I am at the office so I cannot deal with the window cleaner, callers at the door or children's demands for attention.' Then you can decide when you 'leave the office' and step over the boundary line into home life again. However, while it's important to be firm with yourself about getting down to work, it is just as vital that you do not work excessively long hours just because you never actually physically leave the office. Make sure that you allow yourself sensible cut-off points. Overworking can be a problem when there is no-one telling you the working day has ended.

So, whilst there are undoubtedly extra stresses to be coped with in the home working environment, the challenge is to accentuate the positives. Keep reminding yourself about the upsides of being free from the constraints of an office and other people's control. You have greater freedom, but also you have some greater responsibilities.

Chapter 8

Let's talk about your body

In many ways this is the most important chapter in the book because it sets out the physiological reactions to, and the consequences of, stress. When we can control these reactions we have one of the major keys to controlling our physical health. For no matter how intelligent we may be or how many cognitive, sporting or artistic skills we acquire, or how much wisdom, if we cannot protect our bodies we may end up as the most accomplished patient in the hospital ward! Few people realise the damage they may be causing their body when they go into the stress response too frequently.

The stress response

The stress response is actually a wonderful, and necessary, set of internal reactions programmed into the body, designed to save our life. They automatically go into action when the mind perceives some kind of danger or threat. The stress response is also called the 'Fight or Flight' response and, as the name implies, the internal changes it brings about have the purpose of making you stronger to fight or flee your way out of physical danger. For example, if you suddenly realised your house was on fire, you would not sit down with your partner and have a conversation about it, or stand around thinking what to do – you would get out! You would move without thinking. Or, suppose you were out walking in the countryside and suddenly realised that the field you were crossing also contained a bull which then started to charge towards you; your instinctive reaction would be to run, and you would run faster than you ever thought possible. Equally, if you were attacked you would discover you possessed great strength to fend off the attack. This extra strength in an emergency is also documented in many incidents of people lifting cars, fallen trees, or other impossibly heavy objects off someone, thereby saving their life. An automatic response takes over that overrides your logical, frontal brain. You simply take the appropriate action without even thinking what the appropriate action should be.

This is all the work of the 'Fight or Flight' response. It turns you into a 'super-human being', giving you great strength and speed. It is something that has been programmed into you, to help you in an emergency, and on which you can absolutely rely. So this aspect of the stress response is extremely positive and desirable; it must not be seen as the enemy, for many lives have been saved and accidents prevented due to the stress response being triggered.

However, the problem is that the mind often causes this reaction when there is no life-threatening situation. So many of today's threats and difficulties are not physically dangerous but rather present a threat to our emotions, self-esteem or intellectual well-being, and the stress response is actually no help in coping with those particular stresses. In fact, it can hamper our ability to function in the face of these kinds of threats, and this is where it turns negative. What the mind perceives may well be extreme, but if it is not an actual threat to life, all the physical changes that start occurring are a little like revving a car engine when the car is stationary. It's not good for the car and not good for the body either! If we're not going to run or fight, or exert ourselves physically, there is no point having all systems on full alert – it simply wears us out, and worse. When all the body's survival resources are being mobilized as a result of receiving danger signals from the brain, often many times a day, this puts a great strain on the body, which can result in permanent damage or a malfunctioning in some organs or systems. Changes that were only intended to be temporary can become long-term: like raised blood pressure, increased sugar output, reduced fertility and more which is explained in detail below. These then become a health problem.

The 'Fight or Flight' response is an emergency response, meant to be switched on for short periods only, just long enough to get you out of danger. Many people, however, are in this state for too much of the time without realising it because they feel threatened, angry or wound up by numerous everyday situations. This is a natural and useful response in the right context, but when a physical reaction is not appropriate, you have to learn to switch it off.

Below is a description of the changes that take place internally in the 'Fight or Flight' response: the stress response. If you understand what is actually happening inside your body it will be easier to understand why it is important to switch off this response, and put the body back to normal functioning. In my view, it is usually because people don't see the point that they resist introducing changes into their lifestyle. But when you understand the logic, or the science, it should help to motivate you to learn how to switch off this stressful response.

Physiological changes that occur in the stress response

Raised blood pressure and the pounding heart

The heart rate increases to supply more blood, more quickly, to the large muscles that would be needed for quick flight or fighting an aggressor, and to supply the lungs with extra oxygen. This is, of course, highly desirable to make you stronger in an emergency, but not helpful if, for example, worrying about your problems in the middle of the night triggers this response when you need to sleep, or when someone upsets you or cuts in front of you on the road, or when you're facing an important exam, interview or meeting. A rapid heartbeat is not, in itself, dangerous to your health, but because it raises blood pressure it is undesirable for any length of time. If the response is activated too often, it can lead to permanently high blood pressure, which can then lead to a stroke. It is especially bad news to have high blood pressure if you also have high levels of cholesterol in your blood and deposits in your arteries. This puts your heart under strain and any extra stress could push you into the danger zone.

Angry people tend to suffer from high blood pressure more often than those who can remain calm in the face of pressures and problems; if you know this is a particular problem for you, it might be beneficial to your health (as well as your relationships!) to attend an anger management course. In my experience, suppressed anger is the most lethal of all. In my counselling work I have found that many clients who suffer from high blood pressure are unaware they are angry; they discover in the course of therapy that they are suppressing deeply buried anger from the past, usually from childhood, which is creating inner tensions and sapping their vitality. Once they can acknowledge and face those dangerous feelings, they feel a sense of release and relief, which invariably has a positive effect on the blood pressure readings. If you feel this could apply to you, I would strongly urge you to seek out a counsellor, or psychotherapist, with whom you feel safe and comfortable, so that you can work on the anger issue. In addition, if your family has a history of heart problems or poor lifestyle habits, have regular check-ups with your doctor.

Blood clots more readily

The blood thickens due to extra clotting factors being released from the spleen and increased production of red and white blood cells from the bone marrow to provide more capacity to carry oxygen, fight infections and to stop bleeding from a wound. This would be vital in wartime or in a physical accident, but does not help in the mental or emotional battles of daily life. It is not desirable to have thick, sticky blood circulating round the body every time we get wound up. It puts extra pressure on the heart, which can cause raised blood pressure and the formation of blood clots, as well as making you feel fatigued. If you know you go into the stress response frequently, make sure that you drink plenty of water to thin the blood – about 8 glasses or one and a half litres per day. (See Chapter 10 for more information on water consumption).

A note of caution: if you are taking any medication check with your doctor about the implications of increased water consumption, especially if you suffer from epilepsy. Also, learn the relaxation techniques that follow in the next chapter, which put the body back to normal and control all these responses.

Hormonal and chemical changes

Extra cholesterol is produced by the liver when in the stress response to supply long-term fuel due to the stomach having shut down. This takes over from the blood sugar in supplying energy to the muscles. Therefore, keep a careful watch on your diet at times of stress as the last thing you want is anymore cholesterol. Reduce your intake of animal fats and dairy products so as not to overload your blood, which could lead to fatty deposits in your blood vessels, especially your coronary arteries. Excessive cholesterol can also cause hardening of the arteries.

Extra adrenalin is pumped into the blood to enhance the 'Fight or Flight' response and to boost your physical strength. Adrenalin coursing through your veins creates a feeling of hyperarousal, making you feel highly energised, and many people are hooked on this artificial energy but it is tiring for the body and can cause eventual burnout; it also seems to diminish the capacity for clear, rational thinking. Once adrenalin has been kicked into your body you have to be patient until it has run its course. Try not to get agitated about this 'high' or shaky feeling as you will simply pump more adrenalin into your system. I always say, 'Try not to get into a state about being in a state.'

If, for example, you have been woken in the middle of the night by your neighbours saying noisy farewells to their guests, and much slamming of car doors and honking of horns is taking place, try not to get wound up and angry (justified though this may be) or you will still be lying there fuming hours after everyone next door is happily snoring! You must say to yourself in these circumstances: 'Ah well, I have been woken up – never mind, I'll soon get back to sleep, no problem.' You have to fool your mind that there is nothing to worry about; that way you remain calm and peaceful, and will soon slip back into sleep. Just lie, or sit, calmly and practise relaxing all your muscles and the arousal will soon calm down. Remember, it is how the mind perceives something that makes all the difference, and in order to protect your health, your sleep and even your sanity, sometimes you have to pretend to yourself that annoying situations really do not bother you.

Extra cortisol is also released from the adrenal glands as protection from an instant allergy reaction like asthma, and to inhibit inflammation. If elevated long-term, cortisol weakens the immune system, thereby reducing resistance to illness and infection. Healing, which depends on inflammation, is also impaired, and ulcers can result from excessive cortisol secretion. Chronic cortisol elevation also weakens bones and interferes with the liver's ability to regulate fats as well as interrupting repair and growth processes, prioritising instead the immediate gain of saving your life. It is important to realise that long-term health is being sacrificed whenever we switch on the stress response, which is why it is important not to use it unnecessarily and to learn how to relax and switch it off.

There is an increased output of endorphin, the 'feel good' hormone, which is a very powerful painkiller and accounts for people not feeling the pain of a wound until a little time after an accident, a fight or the labour pains of childbirth. However, if the stresses you face are unrelenting and you are constantly triggering the stress response, it seems that the levels of endorphin will reduce, which may explain why emotional stress can cause us to avoid physical stress as we instinctively know our threshold to physical pain is lowered.

The supply of sugar increases

The liver increases the sugar levels in the blood and the pancreas releases increased insulin to metabolise the sugar. This provides a quick short-term energy supply to fight, or sprint from, a perceived threat or danger. If this sugar is used up in some kind of physical exertion all will be well, but if not it places a huge demand on the pancreas to metabolise the sugar overload. It is thought that diabetes can be aggravated, or even started, by excessive demands on the pancreas for insulin. It is very important, therefore, not to indulge in sugary foods or drinks at stressful times unless you are engaging in strenuous physical effort as an excess of sugar will put a strain on your body's coping mechanisms. (See more on sugar in Chapter 10.)

Excessive sweating

When you feel under threat the skin will sweat to cool the underlying, overheated muscles, and to keep the body near its optimum temperature. This response is ideal in protecting you from overheating during a fight, in battle, in running for your life or during competitive sport, but, of course, in a stressful social or business context this reaction is not helpful and simply causes more anxiety. Try reassuring yourself that your sweaty hands, underarms and face could, one day, save your life. This might make you smile to yourself and so relax you, thereby switching off the unwanted adaptation.

Skin turns ghostly white

The colour drains away from the face because of a reduction in the blood supply to the surface blood vessels as it is needed elsewhere (in the lungs, muscles and heart) and also to reduce blood loss from a surface wound.

Heightened senses

We talk about people bristling with anger or indignation and this is literally what happens. When we are alarmed all the hairs on the body stand on end just like a cat's, and although you can't see this reaction, you can sometimes feel a tingling sensation in your skin, especially up the back of your neck. This is a leftover response from primitive days, which is intended to increase your body bulk and make you look more frightening to an opponent or enemy. However, it is not much use in the modern context, when the enemy may be a traffic jam, a delayed train, a cashpoint machine that refuses to function or your PC that has crashed for the fifth time that day – or all of these! Whatever the cause, this response makes you particularly sensitive to your closest environment, which is why, when you are feeling stressed, you often don't want other people too close and you feel hypersensitive. For instance, you may perhaps react more aggressively than usual if someone accidentally bumps into you.

In fact, all of the senses of the body become sharper and more intensely tuned in times of stress, producing increased clarity and focus – a sense of 'aliveness' – the pleasure of which attracts people to engage in high risk sports and other dangerous pursuits. It is also what causes people to produce their best work when under pressure. This heightened alertness, however, although ideal for dealing with a temporary emergency or a dangerous situation, cannot be maintained for long periods without respite. After prolonged stress, the senses seem to burn out and become dulled so that reaction rates slow down. There can also be a tendency to 'switch off' from the outer world, and this can be mistaken for depression, when it is actually exhaustion from hyperarousal. What is then needed is rest from too much stimulation for a while until you feel restored. Try to be aware if your reactions have slowed down after a prolonged period of stress and don't be afraid to admit it to yourself. It could be dangerous in situations where it is essential to be alert, such as when driving any vehicle, using machinery, or any other potentially perilous activity like climbing a ladder to do house repairs or even crossing the road, so just take extra care and extra time for things.

This reaction of intense, prolonged alertness and its rebound consequence of extreme burnout is what used to be referred to as 'shell shock' during both World Wars; the most effective treatment for which was considered to be a substantial period of rest away from any pressures. In my experience, a so-called 'nervous breakdown' is often due to the same cause: an overloading of the nervous system and the senses, inducing chronic hyperarousal which prevents the individual from ever switching-off sufficiently.

Again, a long period of rest and the absence of demands or pressures is the best option for producing respite and cure, and in my opinion, this should be the first line of treatment before drugs or psychiatric methods are introduced. So the possibility of complete exhaustion should be considered when a clinician is presented with patients suffering from nervous conditions. If you feel on the edge of nervous collapse, that you cannot cope with anything, give yourself a rest cure; just do very little apart from eating and sleeping for a week or two, and see if that restores you.

Reduction in libido

The body is extremely pragmatic, so that when facing some kind of threat to its life, it switches off, or reduces output, in all the systems not needed for the struggle to stay alive. Therefore, the body's logic is that if you are in a life-threatening situation, this is not the moment to indulge in sexual activity, and so it shuts down – either completely or partially – all the sexual systems and focuses its resources on where they will be needed most to save your life. As a result of this logic, when under stress you will experience a decrease in libido in both desire and performance caused by a reduction in the sex hormones: testosterone in men and progesterone in women.

This can be the cause of many women's failure to conceive when medical tests have shown there is nothing physically wrong. It can also be the reason for impotence in men. This is frequently the underlying cause of a decrease in sexual desire, all of which can be immensely upsetting when not understood or not explained sufficiently well by your doctor. Many doctors will advise a worried couple to learn to relax and take a holiday together, reassuring them that all will be well. This is good advice, because all the methods of relaxation will switch off the stress response, allowing the body to return to normal functioning, just as long as it is true relaxation and not simply a diversionary activity, like going to the pub or playing competitive sport, which still leaves the individuals tense and wound up. Relaxation usually needs to be taught by an experienced teacher, for although it's a skill that we're born with, most people in the developed world have lost the ability to call upon this natural reflex. In the next chapter you will find a detailed deep relaxation routine.

If you can get away from your usual activities, the more relaxed atmosphere of a holiday will usually work wonders by introducing greater opportunity as well as an increased inclination for focusing on your sex life; provided you are not too emotionally wound up and tense about this problem. Being away from the pressures and strains of everyday life should automatically bring about increased physical relaxation, which will return the sex hormones to normal levels. The effects of relaxation on fertility can be widely observed in reports of the many couples who conceive when they stop trying, sometimes after they have adopted a baby, or after they have just resigned themselves to not being parents. If this is a problem for you and/or your partner, try to be patient. Don't allow it to cause more worry and stress or to damage the relationship. Recognise that it is most probably the result of physical stress responses, rather than a sign that you are no longer attractive to, or sexually attracted by, your mate. Heed the advice above and learn the relaxation techniques I describe in the next chapter.

⅄ Exercise: Holiday at home

Take mini-holidays at home, put your feet up and indulge yourselves unashamedly for two whole days. Leave all mundane tasks until next weekend and 'play'. Enjoy yourselves utterly and completely for forty-eight hours. You'll probably feel 10 years younger on Monday morning, and this could be the beginning of a whole new way of life! If you don't have a permanent partner, just apply the advice in a singular way, and help yourself to relax.

- Switch off your telephone for the weekend or leave the answering machine to take all calls.
- Stock up on your favourite food and drink.
- Get a pile of DVDs to watch.
- Take time to read to each other, maybe a favourite childhood story or a poem, or make up stories – one of you starting it, then the other taking over, and alternating like this until you arrive at the ending.
- Put on music and dance together, perhaps like you used to when you first met.
- Take long, foam-filled baths with sensual oils, have picnics in bed, and see what happens!

Digestive system shuts down

Once again, if the body has received messages from the brain that you are facing a serious threat, it will prioritise against eating a meal in favour of saving your life, resulting in the complete, or partial, shut down of the entire digestive system. This is why your mouth goes dry and it's difficult to swallow when you are anxious or frightened, and you generally lose your appetite as it would be inappropriate to eat when the system isn't working. So, try not to eat when you're stressed because you won't digest your food very well. The digestive juices are needed elsewhere and the blood normally employed in supplying the stomach is diverted away to the large muscles of the body to give you that extra speed and strength. The blood vessels to the stomach contract allowing little blood through, and this is thought to be a possible cause of stomach ulcers. Prior to this, you are likely to experience other digestive disorders such as indigestion, nausea or cramps.

Irritable bowel syndrome is another consequence of this response, due to the fact that your food has not been properly digested and broken down, firstly in the mouth and then in the stomach, giving the bowel too much work to do. This causes excessive contractions of the muscles in the walls of the intestines which stretches the sensory nerve endings, and is painful. Learning to relax will greatly help this condition.

If you are in a stressed state, sit quietly for a few moments before you eat and practise relaxing and breathing rhythmically and slowly (see Chapter 9 for correct breathing) to give your body time to return to normal functioning. This was originally the reason for saying a grace before meals – to introduce a moment of calm, and create a space in which to unwind and let go of the preceding activity. What wisdom! It might be sensible to re-introduce this tradition; in fact, I have friends who do so for the sake of their children as it quietens them down before they eat.

At the very least, try always to create a peaceful space around you when you sit down for a meal. Also try not to eat 'on the run' and avoid arguments during meals. This latter point is especially important with regard to children. If they become upset at mealtimes, they simply cannot eat or digest their food fully. So try to avoid battles about eating, and create a calm, happy atmosphere before and during mealtimes. Do not scold children if they refuse to eat when they are upset for they are instinctively right – they genuinely cannot.

Breathing becomes rapid and shallow

This change facilitates a quick exchange of oxygen and carbon dioxide, which increases the performance of the lungs. This is useful when you have to exert yourself, but not if you are sitting still, perhaps tensed up in a state of anxiety, anger or are hurt.

The altered breathing rhythm can cause panic attacks due to hyperventilation: over-breathing for the activity you are engaged in. If you were running or fighting or exerting yourself physically in any other way, then your oxygen requirement would be greater than if you are sitting still. If you breathe in more oxygen than your body can use, the excess stays in your blood and causes the symptoms often experienced in panic attacks. These are dizziness or light-headedness – as if you are about to faint or as if floating through fog or with your head full of cotton wool – tingling in the hands and fingers and sometimes in the toes, a restricted feeling across the chest or a choking feeling in the throat. This is due to having too much oxygen in your blood and too little carbon dioxide.

An altered breathing rhythm can become a permanent habit, leading to frequent panic attacks and/or constant uncomfortable symptoms like the ones mentioned above. In this case, the individual never feels really well, or fully functioning, and is always frightened that the panic attacks will overwhelm them and possibly cause their death from asphyxia. This won't happen, but the sensations are very unpleasant. It is important that sufferers of panic attacks are taught how to bring their breathing down to their diaphragm and breathe normally again as nature intended. Some people get into a bad habit of holding their breath when under strain and this can also cause similar symptoms. Many sufferers of panic attacks are advised to carry a brown paper bag with them and to breathe into it at the first sign of symptoms. This is good advice as they will then inhale the carbon dioxide they have just exhaled into the paper bag, which restores the balance of oxygen and carbon dioxide in their blood and gradually the symptoms will subside. (Don't breathe into a plastic bag as you could suffocate!)

It is important to recognize when your breathing has become shallow and altered from its normal rhythm. Learning to control and calm your breathing is one of the most important skills you can acquire for the release of stress and upset of all kinds. It is a physiological fact that you cannot feel anxious and breathe calmly at the same time, so learning to breathe correctly gives you the key for controlling your emotional responses. If I could only teach one stress reduction technique, I would teach correct, abdominal breathing, for it is so effective in calming the whole body and mind. (See Chapter 9 for more on this.)

Muscles tense for action

It is mostly the large muscles that tense up in the stress response: those that would be needed for the action of running or fighting, like the muscles in your legs and upper arms, the ones that clench your fists and the muscles in your diaphragm, or solar plexus, to protect against a blow. The shoulder muscles will hunch up, and the buttock muscles may tighten, as might the muscles in the soles of your feet and your toes. Another instinctive reaction is to frown and clench your teeth – to make you look fierce to an opponent! Most people report a feeling of tension first in their shoulders and then in their arms and hands. But if you try to become aware of your entire body when you feel anxious or threatened or wound up, you will notice all the other areas of tension also. Often people are not aware that they clench their teeth much of the time until it is pointed out to them. Many do this in their sleep without realising it until their dentist remarks that they are grinding their teeth away. The same applies to frowning. People are often unaware of it but frowning tightens a band of muscles around the head and can cause headaches.

Tension is tiring. It requires considerable energy to hold muscles in a contracted state. Just try holding your arm out in front of you for about 10 minutes and see how tiring it is – your muscles will ache from the effort. Chronically tense people are generally chronically tired; they are using too much energy to no avail. Letting go of the tension by relaxing and loosening up will remove the fatigue and free that energy for more joyful living. I see people walking down the street with clenched fists and arms held tightly into the sides of their body as if they are afraid their arms would fall off if they let them swing loosely. Some people sit with tightly crossed legs impeding their circulation and with arms folded tensely across their chest, pushing their shoulders up into a hunched position, constricting their breathing. Such a terrible waste of effort!

Furthermore, it is the tension in muscles that sends the alarm messages to the brain via your neural pathways, signalling the need to switch on the 'Fight or Flight' response. So whenever you have excessive tension in any part of your body, not only are you wearing yourself out but you are also activating the stress response and many, if not all, of the above changes. You can, therefore, see why it is so desirable to relax as much as possible and not use more tension than necessary for any task.

It is not surprising that a researcher into the stress syndrome recently stated:

'How we live affects how long we live.'

If you rush about in an aggressive manner getting angry and wound up at the drop of a hat, you are constantly putting your whole system under extreme strain. Of course, if you face a truly life-threatening situation – as in any of the many parts of the world where wars are raging – it is almost impossible to relax; to slip easily each night into unguarded sleep, or to connect inwardly with joy, harmony and calm. But many of us behave as if we are in the front lines of a war zone in everyday life, getting worked up about the smallest things. It is worth considering what it might be like to find yourself caught in the crossfire of warring groups, to risk a bullet every time you go to the shops. That might put our stresses into perspective, and we might stop reacting to someone taking our parking space as if we are fighting for our lives! That outcome really doesn't matter. Why shorten your life for it? Why burn out over little irritations like someone cutting in front of you on the road? Why not just smile and wave him or her on? Chuckle to yourself about the number of times you've done the same to someone else instead of reacting as if they'd just murdered your mother!

In the next chapter I will give you ways of controlling the stress response, or discharging it. I will also introduce you to some simple but effective loosening movements for unwinding your tensions and some ways of relaxing more in everyday living, and finally I offer you a deep relaxation routine to restore you completely.

Physical exertion can also be a good way to let off steam, and sometimes it is necessary to go into action to use up the stress chemicals sloshing round your body. So if you find yourself getting really wound up, with all systems racing, and you can't let go and relax, then go for a run, walk vigorously or run up and down a few flights of stairs. If none of that is possible in the circumstances, go to the cloakroom and jump up and down on the spot and practice some air-boxing or tackle some physically strenuous job. But after you have let off steam and discharged the pent-up energy, do practice some of the unwinding and relaxation exercises from the next chapter. It is always important to relax and unwind eventually, to put your body back into neutral, back to normal.

Chapter 9

Just relax ...

It cannot be said often enough: relaxing your body is the way to switch off the stress response. Relaxation is one of the most important skills to acquire in order to control your stress levels. When we are stressed we automatically tense many muscles, so that learning how to relax the main muscle groups in your body and developing the awareness that tells you when you have tensed up again is one of the simplest, yet most effective, ways of keeping yourself in a good state, physically, mentally and emotionally.

Relaxation switches off the 'Fight or Flight' responses that have been described in the previous chapter. Relaxation instantly releases you, mentally as well as physically, but sadly, many people have forgotten how to incorporate it sufficiently into their daily lives. There is so much pressure in today's world that it's understandable if you feel you cannot take time off to relax, that you must be focused and active at all times or you'll never get it all done. However, if you relieve the pressure regularly by giving yourself some relaxation breaks, then you can take much more pressure in the long-term and, ultimately, you'll achieve the success you desire rather than collapsing from burnout, or any of the stress-related illnesses, with the consequence of being forced into a longer break to restore your health! As you will have gathered from the previous chapter, resting and relaxing your body means less wear and tear on your internal organs because you are releasing your body from the strain of the stress responses, as well as actively assisting the body's repair mechanisms.

Firstly, you can help yourself on a day-to-day basis by being more aware of how much tension you use for all your usual tasks. Many people are wound up tight all the time without being aware of it, holding their shoulders hunched up for no apparent reason or clenching their fists tightly. Remember that tension sends signals of distress to your brain that will switch on the emergency responses.

I see so many friends and colleagues using too much energy all the time without recognising what they are doing to their internal organs; even clenching your fists for a few minutes can raise your blood pressure! So imagine what is happening when you hold the telephone too tightly all morning, when you grip the paper you're reading with all your might, when you have your arms tightly folded across your chest for an hour or two during a meeting or have your hands clasped tightly together all evening watching TV, or when you tense up doing DIY or gardening, gripping the paintbrush or garden trowel more tightly than necessary.

Experiment with how much effort you need for your various tasks and then watch yourself in your daily actions and try to become more aware of how much effort you are using. Is it the right amount, or is it too much? Try to use only the minimum amount of tension (or tightness) necessary for the task in hand; do not put excessive effort into it.

For example:

- How tightly do you hold the steering wheel when you are driving? Do you have the right amount of tension in your grip to control the wheel, or are you using more effort than required? Do you grip it so tightly that your knuckles turn white?

- Do you clench your teeth? We don't need the muscles in our jaw to drive a car. Nor, indeed, do we need to clench our teeth to read a report, listen attentively or think! However, we often have them tightly held and many other unnecessary muscle groups as well. This is very tiring and wastes your energy.

- How much effort do you use in: washing up, vacuuming, ironing, making your bed, washing yourself or shaving?

- How much effort do you use opening doors?

- How tightly do you hold the telephone? Do you grip it as if it were a 10 ton weight?

- How tightly do you hold the knife to cut or butter a slice of bread, or your knife and fork when eating?

- How many muscles do you use when you are keying into your computer? Are you clenching the muscles in your toes, thighs, stomach or forehead? How many unnecessary muscle groups are you using which could remain relaxed?

- How tightly do you hold your pen to control it across the page? Does tightening your grip help you to write faster, or make you more creative? Of course not, it merely tires you more quickly than necessary, makes your hand ache and switches on the stress responses.

- Do you hunch your shoulders when sitting at a keyboard, when playing a musical instrument or painting – or just most of the time?!

- Do you frown when concentrating or when playing games like golf, tennis, board or computer games?

All of this extra tension is frittering away your valuable energy and winding you up internally. Check what is happening in your body right now as you read this. Is there unnecessary tension in your stomach, your feet, your toes, your legs, your neck, your shoulders, your arms, your hands and your jaw? Keep checking yourself many times each day so that you gradually become more aware of which parts of your body you habitually hold onto or hold in tension.

Pace yourself: balance doing and non-doing

Total relaxation happens when your muscles are doing nothing, are completely still and resting. Further on in this chapter I shall give you a routine for putting your body into a state of deep relaxation, to use whenever you have run out of energy or when you feel anxious and wound up. In a deeply relaxed state the body can replenish itself more completely and calm down all the racing systems, as well as the anxious mind. Deep relaxation allows the body to restore correct internal balance and homeostasis. For example, medical research indicates that the immune system is enhanced when we are deeply relaxed – that is, with muscles totally resting and with all bodily systems slowed down. Other repair and regeneration processes have also been found to be increased when we are in a state of deep relaxation.

You could think of it like this: when we are active, we use ourselves up; when we relax completely, we build ourselves up.

There are two metabolic processes in the body: the catabolic and the anabolic. The catabolic process is the wearing down, and using up, of our bodily systems, and is in action when we are. The anabolic is the opposite process, and is responsible for the maintenance, repair and re-building of our body; it is brought into play when we sleep, meditate, rest or relax. It is obviously important that we spend sufficient time in the anabolic state.

Tense muscles use energy and give off a waste product. This waste is acid in nature, and when we continually push ourselves beyond the point of natural fatigue the result can be too much acid in our system; this can be the cause of aching muscles and joints. The antidote is rest and relaxation. A relaxed muscle is resting, conserving energy and causing no waste, and will switch the metabolism into anabolic mode. However, being more relaxed in all your movements, even whilst working, can help you save energy and therefore you will have more available to you for longer periods. You will also feel healthier due to having a more alkaline interior state. Try to apply maximum relaxation and minimum tension to everyday tasks. In the words of Plato:

'Maximum work with the least effort equals grace.'

Tension overdraws your energy account

Tension often becomes a bad habit that creeps up on you gradually until you literally cannot relax because you have lost the natural ability to let go. Many people run their energy accounts on permanent overdraft, wasting their precious energy by being tense when they appear to be doing nothing (and when they could be relaxing). For instance, when they are watching television, sitting reading, are in the cinema or even when asleep and they are holding muscles in tension. Therefore, even sleep does not restore their energy loss, and habitually tense people are usually chronically tired, always over-drawing on their body's energy supplies of fuel and oxygen.

Relaxation and tension are opposite states, and ideally we need a balance of each. Think of relaxation and tension as two ends of a pole, like a see-saw, balanced on a central point – like this:

Relaxation	X	Tension
Passive	Δ	Active

Figure 3: Balancing point of relaxation and tension

If you tip too far towards either end for too long you need to spend sufficient time at the other end to redress the balance. Too much activity and tension is exhausting, and too much relaxation and passivity can cause feelings of lifelessness, stagnation, depression or powerlessness, which are just as stressful as too much pressure. Having too little to do can be as much of a problem as having too much to do. Ideally, we all need a creative balance of both sides of the pole. This does not necessarily mean an equal amount of time at each end, because this is not always possible, but if you have been at the active, tense end for long unrelieved periods and have become severely depleted of energy, then you will probably need an equally long period at the resting, passive end to restore you and put the balance right.

People recover their vitality at different rates, so it is always important to listen to your body and heed the messages it is sending to you. You may worry that you will never get back into activity if you relax, and certainly sometimes, if you are very tired, you may feel more exhausted after you've relaxed for a while, but this is simply because you are getting in touch with what is actually your true state at that time, and it indicates that in fact you need more rest. Generally, after a spell of relaxation you will feel released, re-energised and refreshed.

If you do not have enough to do and you are not suffering from too much activity, you could still find yourself wound up and tense too much of the time, often through the frustration of insufficient occupation. In this case you will need to balance things by taking more exercise and finding ways to introduce more activity into your day. The loosening and stretching routine outlined later in this chapter will give you a starting point. The best formula is a little of one side of the pole, balanced frequently with a little of the other, to keep the balance from tipping too far towards one extreme.

It may be worth taking a lesson from the heart: an organ that is designed to last a lifetime. The heart is an 'all or nothing' organ: it is either working, or resting – it beats and rests, or contracts and relaxes continuously – and the healthy heart rests for slightly longer than it works. I think this is an example for us to follow if we want to last a lifetime too!

Tension is tiring

Tension is, of course, necessary to perform any action. When we function efficiently we use the right amount of tension for the task in front of us, but when we are feeling stressed or under pressure we usually tense up tighter and tighter in an effort to try to cope more effectively. Up to a certain point, extra tension can improve performance, but more and more tension eventually becomes counter-productive and results in exhaustion.

The Human Function Curve explains this very well:

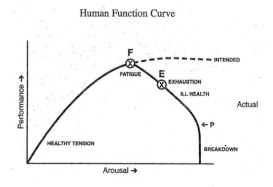

Figure 4: The human function curve (© Dr P. G. F. Nixon, reprinted with permission from Susan Nixon)

In figure 4 the performance curve illustrates that increasing tension, or effort, can also increase your performance – up to a certain point: point F. The F stands for fatigue, and once we have reached this point it is generally useless to continue because our performance, or coping ability, begins to deteriorate. We often imagine we are still functioning well, continuing onwards and upwards towards our goal and maintaining our intended level of performance, which is indicated by the broken line. But this is illusory. The real performance actually begins to deteriorate into a downwards slope, illustrating that the more fatigued we are the less capable we become. The performance level drops off, and things we could do quite easily when rested require extra effort when we are tired. Struggling to maintain the intended level of performance hastens the downhill course and if you persist in pushing yourself on you will eventually reach point E, which stands for exhaustion.

Many people hover between point F and point E much of the time, and they may experience frequent minor illnesses like colds or flu in this state, nothing serious, but an indication that the body's resources are depleted, that you are 'run down'. At point E – in a state of extreme tiredness or exhaustion – you begin to lose the ability to discriminate between the essential and the non-essential: between what needs to be done now and those things that can wait, so you are usually trying to do everything, in a 'headless chicken' kind of mode. If this state continues, with insufficient time for rest and relaxation to provide recovery, the individual descends to point P, which indicates the likelihood of a more serious breakdown of health. The bottom line explains why this should be so. There you will see that the arousal level for internal bodily systems increases the more fatigued we are. In other words, it takes more and more effort to keep an exhausted body functioning and this eventually results in some kind of breakdown of function.

The successful way to function is to put in as much effort and tension as necessary until you feel tired. At that point (F) stop for a while and relax, reduce effort, rest, practice deep relaxation or sleep to restore your resources and your ability to cope. Functioning in this way means you always have sufficient energy and never push yourself onto the downwards slope. Don't get caught in the vicious circle explained below, and don't rely on cups of coffee or alcohol to keep you going when your body is sending you messages of fatigue!

Caught in a vicious circle

A vicious circle can be set in motion: the more exhausted you are, the fewer resources you have to cope, so life can then begin to seem threatening and overwhelming. You therefore tense up more tightly to fight the perceived threat, becoming more depleted the longer this continues. The more fatigued you are, the more life's demands seem like threats; the more relaxed and refreshed you are the more life's demands will seem like interesting challenges to your creativity and resourcefulness.

It is vital to learn to cut through this vicious circle and switch off the racing mind and unhealthily aroused body. Unrelieved tension and pressure will sooner or later result in breakdown of either physical or mental health – or both. It may not be dramatic at first, but if you continually push yourself too hard, you will gradually notice that your efficiency level has deteriorated and you cannot achieve as much as you used to. In fact, everything begins to feel like a strain as you find it harder and harder to cope. This is a warning signal. When most of the things you face each day feel a strain to deal with, you have reached a dangerous level of fatigue, and must take time off to reassess how you are living your life. You can push yourself occasionally, but not as a way of life.

You cannot sprint a marathon, and life is a marathon! Therefore, you need to pace yourself in order to thrive happily right up to the end.

A comedian at the Edinburgh Festival echoed this thought with the following ditty:

> *It's a marathon*
> *It's not a sprint*
> *It's a dance*
> *It's not a race!*

𝕏 Exercise: Escaping the vicious circle

Copy out the lines above and pin them up where you will see them frequently. You could also copy out the Human Function Curve and put that up in some obvious place, and just keep checking where you feel you are on the curve. It is a very useful barometer for a quick check on the state of your life. Try to stay on the up-curve, but if you do tip over the top, then rest as soon as you can, or practise the deep relaxation routine at the end of this chapter and bring yourself back into the healthy tension area.

How to release tension at regular intervals

The routines outlined on the following pages will help to reduce tension levels from moment to moment, and from day-to-day, by unwinding your muscles and loosening you up. Practice these simple movements at regular intervals, stretching out those tightly-held muscle groups to help them relax.

Try all the movements to begin with whenever you recognise that you've tightened up, or if you've been in a static posture for some time, and then pick out the ones that are most beneficial and work best for you. A good time to use some of them is before you go into an important meeting or event, as they really do relax you and will free up your thinking as well.

These loosening movements, calm diaphragmatic breathing and the deep relaxation routine are also on my CD (details of which are on p. xviii).

Loosening and stretching routine

Head and neck movements

This is very good for loosening you when you've been sitting at your PC for long periods. I also often do this one a couple of times when sitting in the bus or train, pretending I'm looking out of the window at something behind me. Do make sure you are not clenching your teeth – this applies to all the movements.

Figure 5: Neck stretch

- Stretch your neck muscles by turning your head to the right, looking over your right shoulder. Feel the stretch on the opposite side of your neck and hold the position for a few seconds.
- Turn to the left, looking over your left shoulder and hold again, feeling the stretch. Keep your body facing front.

- Repeat six times each side, turning your head as far as feels comfortable; don't strain.

This is a good one to practice when stopped at traffic lights or in a traffic jam.

Figure 6: Head tip

- Tip your head over towards your right shoulder, keeping your head facing forwards. Hold for a few seconds and feel the stretch in the muscles on the opposite side.
- Now tip your head over towards the left shoulder. Again, hold for a moment and feel the stretch in the muscles on the opposite side.
- Repeat this movement about six times each side.

The next exercise is useful in stretching your vertebrae in the back of the neck. They become compressed with the weight of the head always pushing down on them and need frequent stretching and releasing. It is only when the head is supported that the neck muscles can fully relax, so they work very hard all day. When you are sitting at home, try to have your head supported by the back of a chair or by a cushion placed behind your head to rest the neck muscles. A headrest in the car is also restful for neck muscles.

- Tip your head out and forwards, and feel the stretch in the back of the neck and in the upper part of your back. (This may make you yawn, which is a very good sign, it means the energy is shifting.)
- Now tip your head out and backwards – not too far, as this squashes the upper spine too much.
- Feel the stretch in your throat and jaw area and let your jaw hang down loosely, don't clench your teeth.
- Repeat these movements about six times each and always finish on a forward one so that the vertebrae in the back of the neck are nicely stretched.

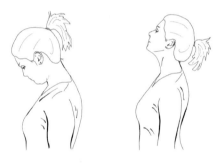

Figure 7: Neck tilt

Shoulders

- Circle your right shoulder backwards six times and then forwards six times.
- Circle your left shoulder backwards six times and then forwards six times.
- Circle both shoulders backwards four times; this should leave them less rounded and not hunched up.
- Shrug your shoulders up and then let them drop. Do this a number of times and register what it actually feels like to drop your shoulders. Drop them many times a day. Then

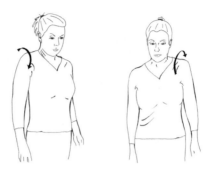

Figure 8: Shoulder release

pull them down a little further and feel the muscles stretching. Much tension is carried in our shoulders and neck muscles, which is very wearing.

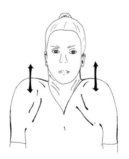

Figure 9: Shoulder shrug

Practice these shoulder movements frequently through the day wherever you are: at your PC, standing beside the fax machine or photocopier, waiting for a lift or standing in a queue at the supermarket. Instead of fuming at getting held up anywhere, be thankful for an opportunity to unwind and stretch your tightly held muscles.

S – T – R – E – T – C – H

- Stretch at every opportunity! If you have been sitting in a static position: at a keyboard, on the telephone, reading, in a meeting, in your car or watching television, have frequent stretches.
- Stretch out your arms and your hands, especially your fingers and thumbs.
- Try stretching your arms out at either side of your body, away from your body, and then stretch your hands backwards almost at right angles to your arms. Feel how good it is to stretch out muscles that have been contracted or static for long periods.

Figure 10: Stretch!

Legs and feet

- Stretch your legs and feet if you have been sitting for any length of time. Get up if you can and shake your legs the way you see swimmers and athletes loosening up before a race.

- Jog on the spot to get some movement into your legs in a small space (you can even do it in the loo!). It also enlivens your whole body and is a good way to wake yourself up if you've started feeling sleepy.

- An actress friend of mine jumps up and down a few times just before she goes into an audition: she maintains it puts colour in her cheeks, a sparkle in her eyes and makes her feel alert. I sometimes use this warm-up exercise before an important meeting (you can do it in the lift) or even before I am about to see a client when I know I am going to have to sit for a while.

- If you cannot stand up, then just move your feet about; this is important to do when you're sitting at a desk all day. Point your toes up towards your knees to stretch your calf muscles and then push your toes down as hard as you can to stretch your shin muscles. (If you suffer from cramp, don't hold this movement for too long.)

The leg movements below are particularly important for older people who often spend many hours sitting still and can develop leg ulcers if circulation becomes too sluggish. All are especially good if you're sitting in a plane for long periods so as to avoid the problem of deep vein thrombosis. All of this equally applies if you are travelling on a long coach journey.

- Keep moving your feet and legs at regular intervals to ensure good blood circulation. Stretch your entire leg by pushing your heels away from you.

- Circle your ankles, first in one direction, then the other, to help your circulation.

- Again, if you are in a confined space such as a plane, lift each knee up by alternately lifting each foot off the floor a few times.

Arms and hands

- If your hands have been held in a tense position for a while, bent over a keyboard, holding the telephone or the steering wheel of your car, or while washing up, writing, painting or playing a musical instrument, then shake them frequently, as if you had just washed them and had no towel. Pretend to shake them dry – shake vigorously to dispel the tension.

- Stretch the fingers and thumbs out straight and hold for a second or two. This relaxes the hands very effectively and makes them more supple and dexterous. Do it often throughout the day; try to do it between different tasks and also during certain activities. For example, shake one hand whilst holding the telephone with the other and then change hands.

- When you're walking along the street shake your hands from time to time just to ensure they are not tightly clenched. Also, wiggle your fingers frequently to relax them.

- To reduce tension in your arms, shake them in a rotating movement, the way a swimmer does when limbering up before a race. Feel the shake or wobble going all the way up into your upper arm. This can be done standing or sitting and is a good movement to do frequently if you're sitting at a computer all day. It's very releasing.

- When you're spending long hours working on your PC or laptop, practice all these movements as often as possible. Practice the stretching of your arms and legs, combined with the shaking, especially when your arms and hands have been held in a fairly static position for some time. Sitting still is just so unnatural for our body, and it needs all the help you can give it.

The next group of movements are best done standing up.

- Swing your arms backwards and forwards rhythmically. Swing them up in front of you to shoulder height then let them drop as you relax them, and experience the feeling of your arms dropping with no tension in them like a rag doll. Keep up this movement for about 8–10 swings to release tension in the arm muscles and your upper back. This is a good exercise to do while waiting for the kettle to boil or when standing by the photocopier. When talking on the phone, you could swing one arm for a few moments then change the phone into the other hand and swing the free arm. Just fit all these movements in between and around your everyday activities. This way you transform stressful occurrences like incessant telephone calls into relaxing exercises.

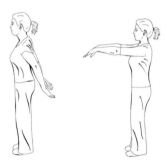

Figure 11: Arm swing

- Twist your body from side to side from the hips, swinging your shoulders round to the left and right a number of times, letting your arms hang down loosely and swing round your body with no tension in them. This is the sort of movement you might see a child doing in the park just for the fun of it. Get back into that child-like sense of being entirely in the present moment, not thinking of what has to be done next, but simply standing and swinging your body and arms. You could even hum a little tune to yourself!

Figure 12: Body twist

- Stretch your arms full out and then circle them backwards about eight times; feel how this large movement helps you breathe more deeply. It is very releasing if you've been sitting still for some time.

Figure 13: Arm circle

- Next, circle your arms forward about eight times: this stretches your upper back muscles and the muscles around your shoulder blades.

Y – A – W – N

- Yawn as often as possible! It is very good for you. When the body yawns it is trying to gain more oxygen. The oxygen we take in when we breathe is our most important source of energy. We can do without food for days but we can survive without oxygen for only two minutes; yet so many people hold their breath much of the time, or breathe shallowly in the upper chest, and therefore receive insufficient oxygen to support them in their activities. People often yawn when they start to relax as their breathing is suddenly freed from the tightness of their chest; this is a good sign. (There is more on breathing below, and at the end of this chapter; also see pages 167–179.)

- One way to make yourself yawn is to push your chin down towards your chest and breathe in deeply through your nose, keeping your mouth closed. You will feel a lovely deep yawn starting at the bottom of your lungs and gradually rising up your chest, expanding your ribcage outwards until it reaches your mouth and is expelled.

- Smile! It is amazing how much better you feel if you put your mouth into a smile, even when you think there is nothing to smile about. It has a psychological effect but it also affects your face muscles and relaxes them. Just try frowning and experience how tight your face feels, then smile and notice the difference. (You use far more muscles for frowning than for smiling.) An added benefit is that when you relax muscles your blood vessels dilate (widen) increasing blood flow – in this case to your brain. So, when you smile your brain receives more oxygen and nutrients with the increased blood supply, which helps you think more clearly.

Breathing

- Whenever you have to perform any action or activity that's a bit of a strain, always breathe out at the moment of greatest effort. Most people breathe in when making a physical effort, but you should use your breath to assist you and this is achieved by breathing out – not in – and not by holding your breath. The exhalation gives you extra strength; you have the force of the breath behind the effort. Don't forget to breathe in first, of course, but do not hold your breath as this will increase the strain on the body. Calm, diaphragmatic breathing is outlined at the end of the chapter.

- Use any annoying situation as an opportunity to remind yourself to unwind. If you are kept waiting by a colleague, friend, your children or your partner, don't get wound up, simply stretch and let go. Think of it as putting yourself back into neutral in a resting state, ready for action when needed and not tense.

Let irritating situations be your triggers to stretch, unwind and let go. Allow the relaxation response to take over from the stress response – and lengthen your life!

Massage

It is wonderful to receive a massage from someone else, either a professional or one's partner, because massage helps to loosen tightly-held muscles and encourages them to release their waste products more completely. This is mainly lactic acid, and when there's a build-up of toxic waste, muscles often feel very sore when touched. Once they relax, however, the waste can be carried away by the increased blood flow – another very good reason to release the tension at every possible opportunity.

- Aromatherapy is a particularly therapeutic form of massage because of the wonderful fragrant essential oils that induce a calm and relaxed state of mind, as well as of body, and they really do work! Other forms of massage which developed in the East are now available almost everywhere, such as Japanese shiatsu, Reiki, and Do-In, which is a form of self-massage based on pressure points similar to acupuncture, combined with yoga postures. It has similarities with reflexology, which is massage of the feet concentrating on specific points, said to relate to different organs in the body. It can sometimes be quite painful, but is very effective at clearing energy blocks and helping in the relief of certain problems. It can also unlock suppressed emotion, which can be extremely healing.

If you cannot persuade your partner and the bank balance precludes booking up with a professional, you can do a lot to help yourself by massaging your shoulders and neck frequently, and also your leg muscles, feet, hands and head.

- Use your fingertips to massage your shoulder, working outwards from where your neck joins your shoulders, in a circular movement. Those muscles at the point where the neck and upper back meet are usually very tense and need a lot of massage and easing out. As they release, you should find yourself yawning again. This is a sign that you are getting more relaxed, and your breath is releasing.

- Massage your neck by tipping your head slightly back to relax the muscles, then take hold of the skin, squeeze and let go, gently working upwards to your head.

- With the fingers of both hands, massage in circular movements either side of your spine, again working upwards from the base of the neck to the base of your skull.

- Now massage firmly across the back of the head, and slowly work your way up the back of your head, moving the scalp as you go until you reach the crown. Massage firmly across the top of your scalp as you do when shampooing your hair. Feel the wonderful release as you move your scalp; this will often unlock tensions in the face as well. You can frequently shift a headache by massaging your head and neck.

- Massage your jaw, making circular movements with your fingertips, letting your mouth hang open. Many tension headaches are caused by clenched teeth and also by continual frowning.

- Massage your forehead by smoothing outwards with your fingertips from the centre towards the temples at each side. Visualise your forehead widening. Then, gently smooth your forehead upwards from your eyebrows to your hairline – feel as if your forehead is getting higher. Visualise all the worry lines being smoothed away. Feel your forehead becoming wider, higher, smooth and calm.

- Massage your thigh muscles by squeezing and letting go and by placing your hands firmly on the tops of the thighs and wobbling the muscles from your groin to your knees, especially just above the knee where a swelling can sometimes develop. Working around this area helps prevent fluid build-up, which causes the puffiness. Then work on down the leg, squeezing and rubbing the shin muscles in the front and gently squeezing and wobbling the calf muscles on the back of the leg.

- A foot massage can be very soothing and will help you to let go and feel at ease with yourself and the world. Gently rub your toes, one by one, especially working around the joints. Massage the soles of your feet with your thumbs in circular movements.

- Massage your hands by rubbing them gently together as if you were rubbing in hand cream, and then with one hand gently massage the fingers of the other hand, one at a time; this feels very comforting.

Deep relaxation routine

When you have mastered deep relaxation you have a powerful antidote to whatever life throws at you. Deep relaxation is an elixir: a supreme remedy for life's disturbances. It is deeply restorative, releasing stress and distress of mind, body and emotions; it puts you back to a state of harmony and assists healing, repair and replenishment of the body's energies. You can practise it anywhere and you don't need special equipment or a trained therapist to assist you. This is your own personal therapy and the benefits are always available to you.

Try to practise the routine outlined below for half an hour every day. Regular practice is important at first so that you become skilled at letting go. It will have a cumulative effect of building more calm into your body and mind that will ripple out into your everyday life. If you do not have my CD, then you could record this routine yourself using a gentle, calm and rhythmical tone of voice, pausing between each instruction, or ask a friend to record it for you.

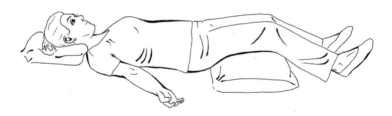

Figure 14: Starting position for deep relaxation routine

● Lie down on a fairly firm surface: your bed or sofa, or on a mat on the floor. Place a small cushion under your head and a large cushion or pillow under your thighs to take the strain off your abdomen and ease the small of your back. Make sure that you are warm as you cannot relax completely if you are cold. It is a good idea to cover yourself with a rug or blanket as your body temperature falls when you relax deeply because your heart rate slows down a little and your blood pressure drops. This is why the regular practice of deep relaxation is especially good for anyone who suffers from high blood pressure.

- Become aware of your shoulders and pull them down towards your hips (the opposite of shrugging), hold them down for a few seconds then let them go. Now feel as if your shoulders are tipping backwards into the support you are on. Tell your shoulder muscles to relax, and just let them go.

- Become aware of your arms. Move your arms a little away from the sides of your body, and bend your elbows slightly outwards. Let your hands rest on your lower abdomen or either side of your body. Now push your arms down into the support, hold for a moment and then stop pushing. Feel your arms getting heavier. Tell yourself to let go more and more through the muscles in your arms. Feel them being completely held by the support. Let go a little more.

- Now be aware of your hands. With your hands still supported, whether beside you or resting on your lower abdomen, stretch out your fingers and thumbs. Hold the stretch for a few seconds and then let your fingers flop. Let them go limp, not holding onto anything or clasped together, and feel your hands completely still and relaxed. There is nothing for them to do right now, just rest. Feel how calming it is to have completely relaxed hands.

- Now be aware of your legs. Push your legs down into the support, hold for a few seconds, and then let go. Let your feet flop outwards. Now, let your legs fall a little more apart and let your knees roll outwards. Feel your legs sinking down into the support. Let go a little more. Feel your legs becoming heavier and completely relaxed.

- Now be aware of your abdominal muscles below the waist. As you breathe out, let these muscles feel loose, limp and easy – no holding on. Now feel your buttock muscles letting go. Feel the whole of your lower body being held more fully and relaxing more completely.

- Now be aware of your diaphragm just above your waist. Feel as if this part of you is expanding slightly. Just let go all around your middle, and feel your easy breathing in this area. Feel your ribcage moving outwards as you breathe in, and feel your diaphragm expanding. As you breathe out slowly, feel yourself relaxing – feel your body letting go more deeply. It is always the out-breath that relaxes you. Take a few moments to experience your calm, rhythmical breathing in your diaphragm – in the middle of your body – exhale a little more slowly than you inhale, and feel yourself letting go more and more deeply on each out-breath.

- Now be aware of your back being supported. Press down a little more heavily into the support, hold for a few seconds, then stop pushing and let go. Feel your whole body being held a little more completely than before. Now let go even more deeply.

- Now be aware of your mouth and jaw. Make sure your top and bottom teeth are slightly apart, not clenched together. Let our tongue rest near the bottom of your mouth, behind your lower teeth: this is the relaxed position for the tongue. Let your lips touch lightly. Become aware of how it feels to have a relaxed mouth and jaw.

- Now imagine a smile beginning in your mouth and slowly spreading into your cheeks; feel as if your cheeks are widening out a little so that the whole of your lower face feels relaxed.

- Now be aware of your eyes. Close your eyelids lightly and let your eye muscles relax – there is nothing to focus on, or stare at. Let your eye muscles rest and enjoy the peace that comes from shutting out all visual stimuli for a while.

- Now be aware of your forehead. Imagine gentle fingers smoothing your forehead outwards from the centre to the temples at either side. Feel as if your forehead is widening. Imagine all the worry lines are being smoothed away. Now imagine your forehead is being gently smoothed upwards from your eyebrows to your hairline. Experience your forehead higher, wider, smooth and calm.

- Now imagine gentle hands are massaging your scalp: up over the top of your head and down the back of your head. Feel as if your whole head area is expanding a little. Let go through all the muscles in your scalp. Imagine any tensions in your head floating away up into the atmosphere. Relax your scalp and head.

- Now just enjoy the feeling of being relaxed. Enjoy the feeling of ease. Rest in the calm and peace that come with letting go deeply and completely.

- Staying in the relaxed feeling, now rest your mind by imagining yourself in a beautiful, peaceful place: a place where you feel calm and safe. Rest in this beautiful place in your imagination for a few minutes. Enjoy this inner picture, and be aware that this is your special place, that you can return to any time you choose.

- Also be aware that this deep relaxation is a very healthy thing to do. You are not wasting your time. You are using time very creatively to restore your energy and vitality and boost all the repair and renewal processes of your body.

- Stay with your beautiful inner picture for as long as you wish to. If your mind wanders off, just keep gently bringing it back to your calm, peaceful image – this is your inner sanctuary. This peaceful experience is always there for you to connect with at any moment you need more calm.

- When you wish to come back into normal alertness, do so gently and slowly.

- First, gently wiggle your fingers and toes; then have a gentle stretch. Stretch out your arms, hands, and fingers; then stretch your legs, feet and toes.

- Push your heels away from you to stretch out your spine and back muscles.

- Roll onto your side for a moment or two and become aware of your outer surroundings again. Then finally, when you are ready, sit up slowly.

- Always return slowly from deep relaxation as all the systems in the body have slowed down and you do not want to shock or strain them. Just sit still for a few moments taking plenty of time to return to your normal, everyday awareness. Then stand up slowly, so as not to feel dizzy. Try to move and speak a little more slowly than you usually do for as long as you can. Just keep that feeling of calm with you for as long as possible.

- Half an hour is an ideal time span for this deep, restorative relaxation, but if you want to drift off to sleep for a short while afterwards that is fine. In fact, you will find that even just ten or fifteen minutes of sleep after completing the full relaxation will be extraordinarily refreshing. This routine is a wonderful way to send yourself to sleep at night but do try to practise it at other times too, to experience its unique benefits, and not merely as a prelude to your night's sleep.

Practising this deep relaxation routine frequently will build more calm into you at all levels, so do persevere with it even if, at first, it is not easy to be still. Don't try too hard, you just have to let it happen. Eventually you will begin to experience the cumulative effect and you will be able to switch into a calm state with ease. Take regular time out to experience how you can alter your internal state. Also see the deep relaxation as a way to pay into your energy account, to build reserves. (This relaxation routine is featured on my CD, see p. xviii for further information.)

Calm breathing

This exercise will restore you to feeling calm and at ease when you don't have time or it's not appropriate to practice the deep relaxation technique. It can also be used to dispel difficult or negative emotions. Whenever you have become wound up and angry or anxious, fearful or stressed generally, you will find this technique is a great help in putting you back in control and restoring your equilibrium. This is the way your body is designed to breathe for normal everyday activities. Practice this routine to become familiar with how correct breathing feels and where in your body you should feel the rise and fall of your breath. In this way you will become skilled at controlling your breathing for when you actually need to calm down. As I have explained on page 167, in the stress response our natural breathing pattern is altered (you may like to re-read the description to remind yourself) and the routine outlined below is the way to return to normal functioning.

This routine can be practised sitting or lying down. If you are sitting, sit well back in your chair, letting the back of the chair support your spine, with your legs uncrossed and both feet on the ground.

- First, breathe out; let your breath out in a slow sigh. Now breathe in slowly, feeling your diaphragm (just above your waist) expand outwards. As you breathe out again, say to yourself, 'Let go', and feel yourself beginning to release the tensions in your body.

- Now breathe in again, feeling your ribcage on either side of your body expand sideways, and now slowly exhale, letting your out-breath be a little longer and a little slower than your in-breath.

- Repeat by inhaling slowly. Experience your ribcage spreading sideways and your diaphragm expanding in front of your body. Never hold your breath once you have inhaled, just let your breath out again in a slow sigh. Pause for a second before you breathe in again, as above, feeling the expansion in the middle of your body.

- Continue this rhythm for about five minutes. Concentrate on making sure that you are breathing into the middle of your body. Feel that part of you expanding sideways and let your out-breath always be a little longer and a little slower than your in-breath.

- Practice at first by counting to three as you breathe in, and to four as you breathe out. Just say slowly to yourself as you inhale: 'In, two, three'. Then, as you exhale, say: 'Out, two, three, four'. Continue for about five minutes. The counting is simply to give you the experience of breathing out for a little longer than you breathe in. If it feels wrong, forget the counting and just focus on slightly lengthening your out-breath. Continue to practise for a further five minutes, so that you get into the rhythm and understand how it should feel.

- Practice this exercise a number of times every day for just a minute or two, so that when you actually need it you will be skilled at calming your breathing and bringing it down to your diaphragm where breathing is designed to take place for ordinary, everyday activities.

- Use this technique to re-establish equilibrium after, or even during, any stressful event or after a difficult or emotional encounter with someone.
- When you have mastered your breathing, try to imagine that you are breathing out any negative emotions.
- Visualise them floating away on your out-breath, and then breathe in positive emotions, to calm your inner state. For example, breathe in calmness, peacefulness and serenity.
- Also breathe out attitudes that are no longer relevant or useful to you; breathe in an attitude that would be more helpful. For example, breathe in an attitude of tolerance, patience, stability or centredness.

As an ancient yoga saying goes:

'When you can control your breath, you will control your life.'

Chapter 10

Food to empower you

'Let food be your medicine' said the great father of medicine, the Greek physician Hippocrates. Good food is indeed the 'medicine' we require for maintaining good health; it is fundamentally what keeps us going. The human body has the most amazing and wonderful design imaginable, and this incredible vehicle – in which we travel from birth to the grave – can surely not be expected to function at its optimum level without the best fuel, anymore than a superb car, or for that matter, a pedigree dog or a thoroughbred racehorse. Does it not seem strange that we recognise the fuel needs of our cars more than the fuel needs of ourselves, or indeed, that we understand how the health of our prize animals depends on feeding them more carefully than we feed ourselves?

The point I am trying to make is that we often don't give enough thought to what we put into our bodies. While we know that the results of using the wrong type of fuel in a high performance car would quickly become apparent, we tend to forget that the results of using the wrong food will also become apparent, albeit in a longer timescale.

Eating the right kind of food is the single most important thing you can do for yourself and your health. The food we put into our body must provide the body with the nutrients it needs in order for it to continue to function. In today's world, many people's bodies are not functioning very well; ill health is widespread, and almost taken for granted. Of course, the pharmaceutical industry is not complaining as it makes enormous profits from poor health. But we should be wondering why hospitals and doctors' surgeries are so full, and why we are spending fortunes on medications to keep us going. It is becoming increasingly apparent that one of the most obvious reasons for this is that we are eating the wrong foods.

It can seem complicated to address the matter of what constitutes a good diet, and in this chapter I shall try to simplify the subject and give you a few tips for maintaining your body at the peak of its powers. For, whilst good nutrition is always important, it is especially so when you are stressed, strained or overloaded.

When we feel stressed or upset we often turn to food and drink which comforts us, but which, in fact, does not really help us physically or psychologically at all. 'Comfort foods' are usually high in sugar and fat content: foods such as crisps, chips, fry-ups, ice-cream, sweets, chocolate bars, cakes and biscuits, as well as high fat and excessively salty 'takeaway' and ready meals. These may give us a quick 'high', but it is not long-lasting; it is always followed by the rebound sinking feeling that takes us down, and so we're tempted to reach for another comfort food and perhaps carbonated, caffeine or alcoholic drinks as well.

Low-quality food of this type creates a huge problem for the body because it does not supply enough of the nutrients necessary for maintaining, repairing and regenerating its organs and systems. It also causes a lot of toxic waste, making us feel run-down and low in energy. We then reach for more sugary and fatty foods to lift us up again, with the vicious circle going round and round, denying us the nutrition we really need in order to feel well and happy. Comfort foods will not harm us too much if we only indulge in them occasionally, but they don't give the body what it needs to produce abundant health and vitality from day-to-day or to withstand stress.

If your body can't utilise the content of your food to replenish its cells and systems, it has to find something to do with the 'stuff' it has been fed. It has two options: to store it, or to eliminate it. Unfortunately, a great deal of this 'junk food' is stored in the body's tissues and it fatigues you. Just as each of us becomes stressed when overwhelmed with too much to do, so the organs in the body can become equally overwhelmed when we present them with too much work in the form of substances they cannot absorb or use. This stresses them and over time can cause them to cease to function adequately, or to break down completely.

For vibrant health and energy we need fresh, living food, rich in vitamins, minerals and other nutrients – bursting with vitality – in contrast to the dead, packaged and processed offerings that proliferate on our supermarket shelves.

Your healthy diet plan

One quick pointer for how to eat healthily is to imagine a huge plate and picture it containing everything you might eat during each day. You would have a good, healthy diet if one half of that plate contained vegetables (preferably both raw and cooked), salad stuffs, fresh fruit, nuts, seeds and herbs. The remaining half would be divided between one third protein (meat, poultry, fish, eggs, beans and dairy products) and two-thirds complex carbohydrates (e.g. wholemeal bread, wholegrains including cereals and brown rice, potatoes, pasta and pulses), together with a small amount of fats. It is more difficult for the body to digest and absorb concentrated foods such as protein and carbohydrates, which should be eaten in smaller amounts. The body can also obtain protein from vegetables and so we do not need large quantities of meat or dairy produce.

The best things to eat at the beginning of the day are fruit, yogurt, porridge, muesli or a wholegrain cereal with skimmed milk, soya milk or rice or almond milk and little, or no, sugar – use honey instead – or some wholemeal toast or crispbread with low-sugar spread, or Marmite or Vegemite. Traditional, fat-drenched fry-ups are not healthy and make you feel sleepy!

The heavier foods take more energy to digest, and if consumed at breakfast, or in the middle of the day, they will make you feel very tired due to your body using up the energy you need for your day's productivity. Digesting a large three course meal uses more energy than almost any activity you might engage in, apart from mountain climbing or strenuous sport. For this reason it is not desirable to eat a huge, cooked breakfast.

Try to ensure that one meal per day (preferably at lunchtime) consists of a large salad, containing as many uncooked vegetables as possible, as well as all the obvious salad ingredients, accompanied by perhaps a jacket potato, hot or cold new potatoes, rice or lentils and a small amount of animal protein such as tuna, grated cheese or cottage cheese (which has less fat content than other cheeses), an omelette or chicken or if you are vegetarian you could add a veggie burger, some nuts and seeds or tofu. You could also add some cooked vegetables as well. With this combination you will be giving yourself an excellent range of nutrients and a plentiful supply of vital energy to cope with the rest of the day. Keeping your lunchtime meal as light as possible means you'll avoid that middle-of-the-afternoon sleepy feeling.

In the early evening, or at weekends when you can rest afterwards you could indulge yourself with the heavier foods such as pasta, roasts, curry and rich sauces, as well as occasional pastries or puddings. Try to wean yourself off the sugary, unhealthy foods. They are only a habit that it's possible to break if you so desire. (See below for more on sugar.) It takes between 3 and 4 hours to digest a large meal, so try not to eat a heavy meal just before retiring to bed.

Protect your body from free radicals

It is important to protect our bodies from free radicals. Free radicals are harmful oxygen molecules that accumulate naturally in the body and damage healthy tissues. They cause changes in cells that can lead to cancer, heart disease and other serious conditions, as well as being responsible for ageing. To fight back against free radicals you need plentiful supplies of antioxidants that are contained in certain foods and which either stop the formation of free radicals, or disable them before they can do any harm in the body.

Research studies suggest that the more antioxidants we consume in our diet, the less likely we are to die of cancer. The most studied and most powerful antioxidants are vitamins C and E and beta-carotene, which is found in the many fruits and vegetables in the colour range from yellow to rich orange and red hues, such as carrots, tomatoes, red and yellow peppers, apricots and cantaloupe melons (especially rich in both beta-carotene and vitamin C), as well as carotenoids found in dark green, leafy vegetables like broccoli, parsley, watercress, cabbage, kelp, Swiss chard, kale and spinach. Antioxidant properties are also found in green tea and to a lesser extent in black tea.

Below are some essential guidelines for eating for health and powerful energy.

Reduce the sugar

In the stress response, your liver releases extra sugar into your blood (see page 161). It is worth remembering this when you reach for that sugary 'treat' to uplift you. An overload of sugar causes an acidic environment in your body, which will, in fact, fatigue you as the body uses energy to neutralise the acid. Also the initial 'high' from sugary foods or drinks wears off very quickly and will be followed by a sudden drop in energy, making you feel 'low' and empty, so that you'll rush for another quick energy fix. Too much sugar consumption can cause depressed moods as the sugar provides you with no nutritional value whatsoever, offering instead merely empty calories, which are not satisfying in the long-term. Sugar gives you energy for physical exertion, but if not used up in some form of exercise, it will be stored as fat. High sugar intake puts a strain on the pancreas for extra insulin, which can lead to malfunction, and is thought to be a contributing factor in the onset of diabetes. Sugar also encourages the growth of fungal problems and yeast infections like Candida Albicans and thrush. By reducing the sugar in your diet you also reduce the risk of coronary heart disease. Sugar is now considered more dangerous for your heart than animal fats.

We need a certain amount of sugar, but this can be obtained from vegetables and fruit. Do go easy on the fruit though as eating too much fruit can cause sugar overload. Check labels for hidden sugar in foods such as cereals, tinned fruit and tinned vegetables, bread, sauces, baked beans and tinned soup. Especially avoid giving children sugary foods as a treat. It sends the wrong message and starts the sugar habit. If you want to buy sugar at least buy unrefined, raw cane sugar as this retains the trace minerals and some other nutrients which are removed during the refining process. But keep sugar consumption to a minimum, and remember that carbohydrates are converted into sugar in the body.

Reduce the fat

Fats should not be cut out of our diets altogether as they play a crucial role in our bodies, and getting none at all can result in nutritional deficiencies. The key is to consume healthy fats, not the artery clogging ones. Approximately 20% of your calories should come from healthy fats; these are the essential fatty acids (EFAs) that are the building blocks that strengthen cell walls and are necessary for the absorption of the fat-soluble vitamins A, D, E and K, as well as for building a strong immune system, producing hormones and binding to and eliminating acids. Most oils contain both monounsaturated and polyunsaturated fats, and those that are predominantly monounsaturated, like olive oil, as well as raw nuts and avocados, are very beneficial. Oily fish such as salmon, mackerel, sardines, herring and tuna contain the essential omega-3 oils that protect against heart disease, strokes and high blood pressure, lubricate joints, relieve arthritis and some behavioural disorders, as well as improve brain function. If you are vegetarian, nuts, seeds and avocados are all good sources of omega-3s and omega-6s, as well as oils such as linseed (flax), borage, evening primrose, grape seed and hemp.

It is saturated fat (animal fat) that is harmful to your health when eaten to excess and should make up no more than 10% of your daily calorie intake. Use olive oil instead of butter or lard, especially for cooking as it does not oxidize when heated, which other vegetable oils do, producing harmful free radicals. Olive oil should be virgin and cold-pressed, and is delicious drizzled over vegetables and pasta dishes, or baked potatoes, instead of butter.

However, it is very fattening, so consume in moderation. Fats contain approximately twice as many calories as carbohydrates and proteins. All oils should be refrigerated to prevent them from turning rancid, another cause of free radicals. In the fridge they will solidify, therefore you have to remember to remove them from the cold a short time before cooking begins but don't leave them out for too long.

Saturated fats found in red meat and dairy produce are particularly harmful when you are in the stress response, due to the body's production of extra cholesterol and free fatty acids to aid you in 'Fight or Flight' (see Chapter 8). Grill, bake or steam foods rather than frying, and remember the hidden fats in food like pork, breast of lamb, chicken skin, sausages, bacon, egg yolks, gravy, cheese, puddings, cakes, biscuits and pastries and chocolate (although chocolate contains flavonoids, also found in red wine, should be considered good for heart health as well as being mood boosters, but should be consumed in moderation). Avoid foods containing hydrogenated fats, or trans-fats, as these are artificially altered oils which the body cannot utilise and which contribute to the build-up of fatty deposits in your arteries. Processed and cured meats like salami, bacon, ham, prosciutto, sausages and hotdogs are considered potentially harmful to health, and recent Health Protection Agency advice is to eat very sparingly, if at all.

How much salt?

Most people overload their bodies with far more salt than desirable for the body's healthy function. The recommended amount is no more than 6g of salt (sodium chloride) over the course of a day; (this amounts to 2.4g of sodium so check whether it states salt, or sodium, on food labels). Strenuous exercise and excessive sweating in hot weather could increase your salt needs slightly due to some being lost in your sweat, but just remember that too much salt can damage your kidneys and cause high blood pressure, strokes and heart failure. Fluid retention can also be caused by a diet high in salt, and this will contribute to premenstrual tension and could cause serious problems during pregnancy.

Cut down on salty snacks like salted nuts and crisps, and savoury or cheese biscuits. Hard cheeses have a high salt content, as do most tinned and processed foods, especially processed meats, which have recently been declared harmful to health by the Health Protection Agency who advise minimal consumption, as explained before. Try not to add extra salt to your food at mealtimes and use small amounts when cooking. Enhance flavours with herbs, lemon juice or lime juice, or spices like ginger, cumin, turmeric, coriander, cinnamon, nutmeg and chilli when appropriate. Especially ensure children's diets do not contain high levels of salt, and always check food labels on baby foods.

If you are taking any medication, it may not be desirable to reduce your salt intake. In the case of lithium it is essential to have some salt in your diet, so always check with your doctor.

Eat more fresh vegetables

Vegetables should be the focus of your diet and should make up the largest part of your food intake. They are the lowest calorie, lowest sugar, most nutrient-rich foods on the planet, and are one of the best ways to combat those harmful free radicals for they contain the antioxidant vitamins and many other important nutrients such as minerals, chlorophyll, enzymes, phytonutrients, fibre and alkaline salts. Alkaline salts help to neutralise acids in the blood and tissues. (See page 220 for more on avoiding too much acid food.) Try to achieve a mix of eating vegetables raw (most vegetables are delicious in their uncooked state) and cooking them. But beware of eating too many raw mushrooms as all varieties contain a compound which is poisonous in large amounts (see below under 'salad foods').

When cooking, use very little water or steam your veg, to avoid losing too many vitamins, and use leftover vegetable water for adding to soups, sauces, stews or as a base for a veggie smoothie drink by liquidising a mix of your favourite raw and cooked vegetables. If fresh vegetables are not available, the best alternative is frozen, as their vitality is preserved by the freezing process. You can see the abundant life in fresh vegetables, which of course, is transmitted into your system when you eat them. If you leave them too long you can observe the life-force literally draining away as they shrivel up. Whenever possible, choose organically grown produce to avoid the toxins of chemical pesticides and fertilizers, which overload the body with chemical waste and require valuable energy to eliminate. Organic vegetables are also generally richer in nutrients due to the soil in which they are grown being less depleted. You should try to eat at least three to five portions of vegetables, both raw and cooked, each day and more if possible.

Salad foods

As cooking destroys many of the healthful nutrients in vegetables it is important to obtain maximum nutritional value by eating salad foods on a regular basis. These will give you great vitality and energy. Some people consider salad to be dull and tasteless, but if you mix a good variety of raw vegetables with all the usual salad foods, the subtle flavours will grow on you. Especially include avocados in your salads, as they are deliciously creamy and satisfying, and a very good source of protein. Then add an interesting dressing, made with olive oil and lemon juice (or cider vinegar) with a little raw cane sugar, mustard and garlic, and you'll have a treat for your taste buds. In the Mediterranean they know how to make salads enjoyable for the palate, largely due to the amount of garlic included. Garlic has great antibacterial properties, as do onions, and will help fight off infections, especially coughs and colds. Garlic has also been shown to inhibit fungal infections and Candida Albicans. You see, we are back to the argument that food is your medicine, as well as simply enjoyable. This is very much the point.

The right food really will make you well and healthy. Another important factor is that salad foods and vegetables have a high water content, which assists in their assimilation and aids your digestion and your elimination processes. Without enough water content in your food you could be subject to constipation.

Caution regarding mushrooms: One reservation here is in the consumption of raw mushrooms as all varieties of mushroom contain varying amounts of the mycotoxin amanitin, which in large amounts will kill you. Cooking is said to destroy this poison so, just to be safe, keep raw mushrooms to a minimum, or preferably, avoid them altogether.

Fresh fruit

Fruit is said to have been the basic diet of our hunter–gatherer ancestors, and it certainly does contain a significant number of nutrients for optimum health: glucose, amino acids, fatty acids, minerals and vitamins. It requires minimum energy for its digestion and absorption and therefore it is easy on the digestive system. Fruit should always be eaten uncooked as cooking also destroys most, if not all, of its health-giving properties. Fruit should also be eaten on an empty stomach, as it is digested very quickly, only remaining in the stomach for about 30 minutes before passing into the intestines. If it is eaten at the end of a meal it will be held up behind the heavier foods and begin to ferment, causing flatulence and indigestion. Ideally, eat fruit first thing in the morning, or between meals, rather than combining it with other foods. Avoid tinned fruit as it's preserved in very sugary syrup. Even fresh fruit has high sugar content, so eat sparingly, and preferably only eat fruit that is in season in your part of the globe. Surprisingly, lemons and limes do not turn acidic in the body but are instead alkalizing foods, so add these frequently to meals, sauces and drinks.

Fibre

Fibre is often lacking from many people's diets, due to consuming too many refined, white flour products, and this can be another cause of constipation. Foods containing fibre are essential for good health, especially when you are stressed because fibre helps your body get rid of toxins and waste. It is difficult for the body to remain healthy if poisons are circulating and toxic waste material is being stored rather than excreted. Fibre is the one food you can eat plenty of because it does not stay in the body; it passes unchanged through the bowels. Eating fibre is like swallowing a sponge as it absorbs undigested food, toxins and excess cholesterol (including the cholesterol produced internally as part of the stress response) and removes these undesirables from your body via an improved eliminatory process. It acts like a broom, cleaning out the intestines.

Foods containing fibre or roughage are: fresh fruit, vegetables (especially raw vegetables), wholegrains like brown rice, oats (particularly good at soaking up cholesterol), wheat bran, millet, rye, barley, buckwheat, muesli (check for added sugar), whole-wheat pasta, wholemeal bread and crispbreads, high fibre biscuits, oatcakes, high fibre cereals like All Bran, baked potatoes, baked beans, seeds, sweetcorn, unsalted nuts and pulses like lentils, peas, mung beans, chickpeas, kidney beans and aduki beans. Sufficient fibre will be obtained from a mixed diet of the above foods.

Alcohol

Alcohol is a depressant although some think it a stimulant due to the fact that you may feel uplifted by a small amount of alcohol initially. But the 'happy' feeling is actually caused by the alcohol suppressing a part of your brain. This inhibits your internal 'censor', the part of your brain that discriminates between right and wrong and that inhibits many impulses. Consequently, you don't worry so much about anything including your own behaviour and problems seem to disappear. Of course, this is an illusion, and the problems are still there next morning – or when you sober up! Alcohol is, in fact, a poison, and in large amounts it can kill you. It also destroys brain cells and puts a strain on the liver, which has to process it. One unit of alcohol takes approximately one hour to be processed by the liver, so take your time between each glass of alcohol. In addition, drink water alongside your alcoholic beverages to dilute their effect. Alcohol also dehydrates the cells of the brain, and this is the cause of the painful head in hangovers; so when you've overindulged drink plenty of water before retiring to bed, and on waking in the morning. Don't drink coffee as a hangover cure as caffeine also dehydrates you. Excess alcohol consumption can lead to a host of other health problems such as cancer, cirrhosis of the liver, atrophy of the testicles in males and the ovaries in women, high blood pressure and stroke, as well as depression and other mental problems.

It is recommended that women drink no more than 2 to 3 units of alcohol per day, and for men the recommended amount is no more than 3 to 4 units per day. In small amounts it will not harm you, and some health benefits have been discovered in moderate consumption. For example, red wine contains antioxidant flavonoids and some research has found that those who consume alcohol in moderation live longer than teetotallers or excessive drinkers. Ideally, keep your alcohol consumption within the medical guidelines and aim to have at least two alcohol-free days per week.

Eat minimally for maximum alertness

When you particularly wish to be at full throttle it is best to eat minimally. Remembering that large quantities of food require large amounts of energy for digestion, it is sensible to free up your energy for a spectacular performance by ingesting small meals. If you have an important meeting during a meal time, eat some long-lasting energy food about half an hour beforehand – like a banana – to ensure your blood sugar level does not drop too low, and then during the encounter just nibble. In this way you keep your adrenalin flowing and your attention alert. You can eat again after the meeting, if you're starving. Don't fall into the trap of overindulging on either food or alcohol and end up finding it hard to keep awake. In fact, studies have shown that those people who always eat fairly small amounts as a way of life tend to be very long lived. Little and often seems to be a better formula than huge meals with long gaps in-between.

Are you drinking enough water?

As outlined in Chapter 8, one of the body's stress responses is to thicken the blood with extra clotting factors, making it more difficult for your heart to pump it around your body. This puts a strain on the heart and raises your blood pressure so drinking plenty of water is especially important when you are experiencing a lot of stress, in order to thin your blood and assist its circulation. As a general rule, even in calmer times, make it a habit to drink about 8 glasses or approximately 1.5 litres of water during each day. Drink a glass of water before retiring to bed and on rising in the morning drink a glass of water with fresh lemon juice (but no sugar) to flush out your kidneys. Have some bottled water in your bedroom so you can have an extra drink if you wake in the night and keep a supply of water with you when you're on the go or at work, especially if you work in a centrally heated, or air conditioned office.

One way to tell if you are drinking enough water is to observe your urine. Except in the morning, when you haven't had fluids all night, it should be very pale yellow or even clear. If the colour is dark you should be drinking more water. If you drive for long periods keep a bottle of mineral water in the car so that you can take frequent drinks. When flying, water consumption is particularly important as the air pressure inside the plane dehydrates you. You will feel less jetlag if you drink approximately one or two glasses of water per flying hour (if you are flying on very long-haul flights reduce that a little). Try not to consume alcohol or coffee in-flight as both dehydrate the body and add to the problems experienced when sitting in pressurised cabins.

Drinking sufficient water will dilute toxins in the bladder and ensure a high volume of urine output, thereby reducing the possibility of bladder infection, as well as helping to avoid kidney stones. If you don't drink enough the body's wastes become too concentrated and form into crystals that can bond together and create the kidney stones. Also, if the cells in your body become dehydrated they draw water from your bloodstream (your blood is 70% water), adding to the problem of thickened blood when in the stress response. Drinking plenty of water will help avoid constipation and will ensure a clearer and more youthful skin – the skin becomes more wrinkled when we don't consume enough water – and when we're dehydrated we feel more fatigued. It is worth remembering that our bodies are 70% water, and that we are losing water constantly through our skin, our eliminatory system and through our breath, therefore it's essential to replenish it frequently. Also, the skin needs adequate supplies of water to regulate body temperature through sweating.

As people age they often lose the ability to recognise when they are thirsty. Therefore, if you are a senior citizen or if you're looking after an older person, try to ensure that taking regular drinks of water becomes a daily habit, even though the sense of thirst may not be present.

However, a word of caution: if you are taking any medication it may be contraindicated to increase your water consumption, especially if you suffer from epilepsy. Consequently, make sure you consult your doctor about the ideal amount of water you should be drinking.

Hints for controlling panic attacks and pre-menstrual syndrome

Not eating for long periods causes blood sugar levels to drop, and this can contribute to panic attacks. When the blood sugar drops below a certain level, the body releases adrenalin to keep us going, and this excess of adrenalin can cause shakiness and the symptoms and feelings of panic attacks. So, if you suffer from panic attacks, never go for many hours without eating. Make sure that you eat something nutritious (not sugary foods) every three to four hours to keep your blood sugar steady. Look at what I have said about disordered breathing on page 167, as this will also give you more explanations about the causes of, and ways to control, panic attacks.

Eating at frequent intervals, especially complex carbohydrate foods like wholemeal bread, wholewheat pasta, buckwheat pancakes, brown rice, oatcakes or rye crispbreads (alongside healthy vegetables) also helps with pre-menstrual syndrome by keeping blood sugar levels stable, which in turn can help to reduce feelings of weepiness, aggression and mood swings. It may also help if you cut down on salt and salty foods when menstruation is due (but check with your doctor if you are taking medication where this is contraindicated, as with lithium, when no salt intake would be dangerous). Sodium, the main component of table salt, causes fluid retention in body tissues, which is already a problem at this time of the month. The resultant bloated feeling can make you much more sensitive than usual, which will increase feelings of irritability and moodiness.

One final power boost

It is said by many nutrition specialists that our bodies were not designed to digest proteins and carbohydrates at the same time, and that eating these two foods in the same meal causes much energy loss, and eventually increased susceptibility to ill health. This is the thinking behind what is known as the Hay Diet, or Food Combining. You might have heard about this healthful way of eating, and you may wish to try it. Briefly, the theory of the system is that protein foods as well as acid fruits, should not be eaten at the same meal with starches (bread, biscuits, cakes, potatoes, pasta, cereals, rice and other grains and sugary foods). Proteins require acid for their digestion, and carbohydrates require an alkaline milieu in which to be assimilated. When we eat both in the same meal the body produces both acid and alkali in our stomachs, but they tend to neutralise each other, with the result that our foods are not properly digested. It is beyond the scope of this book to expound this theory and system of eating in greater detail, but two excellent books on the subject are *Fit for Life* by Harvey and Marilyn Diamond (2004 published by Bantum) and *Food Combining for Life* by Doris Grant (1995 published by Thorsons). You might like to try this way of eating and see for yourself if it boosts your energy levels and health. It also seems to produce a rather welcome side effect of weight loss without trying!

Emphasise the alkaline foods

Another dimension to the Food Combining diet, increasingly being recognised by health practitioners, is that while the body needs to maintain a good acid/alkaline balance in order to be healthy, most Western diets tend to make our bodies too acidic. It is being realised that this excess of acid is what causes disease and the breakdown of health. We should ideally keep the acid/alkaline balance, also known as the pH balance, at 80/20: that is, 80% alkaline to 20% acid, or close to this ratio. Therefore, it is important to be aware of consuming far more alkaline foods than acid ones. It can be somewhat complicated to adhere to this formula, and an excellent guidebook on the subject is *The pH Miracle*, by Shelley Redford Young and Robert O. Young (2009 published by Piatkus).

To simplify this concept: high water content, low sugar foods cause less acidity. High sugar and high protein foods increase acidity. The most acid forming are animal-based foods: meat, dairy produce and to a lesser degree fish, as well as white flour products (which are converted into sugar in the body) and high sugar-content foods, including most fruits. The alkalizing foods are plant-based: vegetables, salad foods, vegetable juices, seeds like poppy, sunflower, sesame, pumpkin as well as sprouting seeds, and in smaller quantities nuts and non-acid forming fruits.

This nutritional approach is supported by a recent extensive study of the eating habits and health of people throughout rural China and Taiwan, compared with the dietary habits and health of people throughout North America. To summarise: it was found that those people eating a mostly plant-based diet were the healthiest and had far fewer of the diseases that we take for granted like cancer, heart disease, high blood pressure, autoimmune diseases, kidney disease, vision and brain disorders, Alzheimer's and dementia, than those populations that consumed a highly animal-based diet. This research has been published in book form as *The China Study* by Dr T. Colin Campbell and Thomas M. Campbell (2006 published by BenBella Books). It is beyond the scope of my book to explain this study in depth, but I highly recommend *The China Study* to anyone seriously interested in maintaining good health through good nutrition. It provides fascinating and some surprising information. It is slowly being recognised that most American and Western diets contain far too much animal protein and sugar.

Basically, the research indicates that we should eat more vegetables, fresh fruit, wholegrains, pulses, nuts and seeds, some fish and monounsaturated oils such as olive oil, rapeseed oil, linseed oil, avocados and nut oils. We should cut down on, and eventually eliminate, our consumption of animal-based foods, especially red meat and processed meats, dairy produce and sugar (including white flour products that are quickly converted into sugar in the body). Wholegrains are better for us as they take longer to break down and so provide slow-release energy, which helps to keep blood sugar levels more stable, but they still create sugar in the body, and so should be eaten in small amounts.

In this chapter I have given general guidelines about the best ways to eat to protect your health and buffer your body against stress. It's not easy to change the habits of a lifetime, but the research certainly indicates that we should all consider more carefully the subject of diet – not in order to lose weight – but in order to live a long life with greater good health.

So what needs changing?

All this talk of what is the best way to eat may leave you a little bewildered as so many of the recent scientific studies are causing us to radically rethink what we should be putting into our body. Changing habits is never easy, and it's always best to go slowly and just change one or two things to begin with. The best way to start is to discover exactly what you are already eating; and so I suggest that you write down everything you have eaten and drunk at the end of each day for a fortnight or even a month if you can keep it up. Carry a little notebook around with you and just jot down everything you consume – including drinks, as well as all the snacks or junk food! You may not like what you see, but you will then have your eating habits in front of you, and once you have realised just what you are actually eating, it should not be too difficult to work out where adjustments need to be made – what you need more of and what you need to cut down on – following the guidelines in this chapter. You don't have to change every-thing immediately, just start gradually improving your diet and helping yourself to better health.

Try not to eat when you are feeling very stressed and wound up, emotionally upset or angry, because you will not be able to digest your food properly. Remember that in the stress response, the digestive system partially or completely shuts down (see page 166), and so eating in this condition may cause you indigestion, and will certainly mean that you do not receive the full goodness from your food. Eat slowly and try to eat 'mindfully' by giving your full attention to what you are eating, rather than trying to do a number of other things at the same time.

Before eating, try to have a few moments of stillness, to calm down and relax; create a beautiful, peaceful environment around you as often as you can, perhaps with candles and soothing music playing. Enjoy your food, take care of your body, and eat for power and health.

Chapter 11

What we can learn from successful people

There are certain things to be learned from successful people about how to achieve to the maximum of one's ability or desire, and how to thrive while doing so. Research into why and how 'top' people cope with the enormous demands on them has revealed some interesting common denominators: the first of these are known as the three Cs.

Control, challenge and commitment

Control

The subject of control has already been discussed in a number of different ways in previous chapters, precisely because it is such a fundamental way of freeing yourself from stress. In the examples below we are not talking about being a 'control freak', always wanting to be controlling of others or of every situation. That is negative control. The sort of control where you constrain, burden or repress others is quite different from positive, empowering control. Positive control is not a constraint so much as an enabler. This can be understood as the kind of control wielded by the director of a play, not that of an autocrat. It is the power to direct, not dictate. It is power 'with' rather than power 'over'. Those who want power 'over' others usually feel powerless inside. What is being discussed here is the importance of developing your inner power.

Here are a few additional points:

- **Adopt a 'can do' approach:** Most successful people thrive on the demands of their lifestyle rather than collapsing under the load largely because they have a strong belief in their ability to control most of what they wish to control. This has been found to be one of the common denominators that exist in all those who achieve any success in life. The people who succeed at whatever they undertake appear to have an inner self-belief and a 'can do' attitude towards life's demands.

- **Enjoy being in control:** Successful people enjoy having control and want to be in control, rather than looking to an outside authority to direct them. Knowing you have a high degree of control engenders a feeling of being 'on top of things', which relieves any feelings of distress, threat or helplessness, reducing the amount of stress involved in any situation, however demanding. The consequence of this means more energy is available for a high level of performance, in spite of enormous responsibility. In addition, when you feel sufficiently in control it is also possible to take time off to relax, which is, of course, healthy self-management.

- **Avoid things you cannot control:** Not having control, or perceiving yourself as having little control over events or other people, is one of the greatest stresses we can face, and will usually switch on the 'Fight or Flight' response in an attempt to battle feelings of helplessness or feeling threatened by events outside of your control. This is very debilitating and can have negative long-term consequences for your health. Because of this, it is wise stress management to avoid, as much as possible, putting yourself in too many situations where you cannot control what is happening or where you cannot have any influence on the people around you.

- **Concentrate on what you can control:** Try to identify those areas where you do have control, and maximise the benefit of those situations by concentrating your efforts on these projects or life areas as much as possible. Most people who arrive at the top of their profession or career have found ways to take control as often as possible in all areas of their lives and to nurture the opportunities for increasing their areas of influence. When you take control even in small ways – such as deciding where to place your boundaries as far as other people's demands are concerned – your self-esteem and confidence will grow; two qualities generally seen in abundance in successful people.

- **Find control outside work:** If you do not have much control in your working life, make sure that you engage in your leisure time in activities where you can feel in control to a satisfactory degree, as a counter-balance. This could be by playing a sport regularly with a friend or a group of friends with whom you feel equal, and where you can control and develop your own performance. Or you might enjoy developing your artistic or musical abilities so that you can feel more in control of your own talents and capabilities. Attending a self-defence class or practising meditation, tai-chi or any of the martial arts can also give you a sense of control, especially a sense of self-control. Rather like the conductor of an orchestra, you can coordinate the many sides of yourself to function in a most satisfying way, so that the areas of stress, or distress, shrink into insignificance beside the fulfilling and satisfactory areas.

- **Monitor your levels of control:** Even if you have achieved considerable seniority in your work life, do keep a check on where you feel un-free, as this is where the stresses intensify. For instance, managers are typically seen as having a significant level of control, but this greatly depends on the hierarchical structure of the organisation. As we have already noted in a previous chapter, middle managers often experience pressure from above and below, and generally experience more stress than those who work under them. However, even where you have certain constraints on your control you can de-stress yourself considerably by choosing consciously to accept those constraints. This choice of accepting the situation rather than resisting it gives you a feeling of autonomy, which is empowering. But, this has to be a genuine choice with which you feel comfortable.

- **Control your reactions:** The one area where we can always have control is in our reactions, whether to external events or other people. We are always free to choose how we interpret something that happens, and then how we decide to react. Of course, it's not always easy to find the inner strength to stand back and take a moment to reflect before we act or react. But by practising the stress management and relaxation techniques throughout this book you will become more able to feel in control of yourself at least, even if not always of the outer world.

- **Structure your free time:** Some people have a high degree of control at work but do not take sufficient control of their free time, thus they often feel anxious at weekends when there is no structure. So manage your leisure time as well: not by being frantically busy, but instead by deciding what you want to do, when you want to do it and when to relax instead of just drifting. Many people become depressed on weekends, or holidays, because of the lack of a framework or purpose. In my therapy sessions men often complain that at weekends they do what their family wants and arrive back at work on Monday mornings feeling un-nourished and un-refreshed, and a little resentful. Women can also fall into the trap of putting their energy into directing their children's lives, or focusing too much on supporting their partner's course through life, giving insufficient attention to controlling and directing their own lives. It is important not to neglect your individual talents and needs for self-expression.

Challenge

Another feature of successful people is that they see life's demands and problems as interesting or exciting challenges to be overcome, not as threats that may overwhelm them. Obviously, whether something is perceived as a threat or a challenge to your ingenuity depends on the resources you think, or feel, you have available. Never forget, however, that the inner attitude with which you approach any situation is a very important resource, and this can be developed and strengthened all through your life. My suggestions throughout this book are aimed at helping you to do just that. Let's focus on this aspect of challenge:

● **See problems as challenges:** Try to work on seeing problems as challenges to be approached from a new perspective. Instead of saying: 'I have a problem', try saying: 'I have a puzzle to solve', and see how different that feels. The next time you feel threatened by a problem or difficult situation, think of it as a game you have to play. Enjoy working out your strategy for solving the puzzle, or winning the game. You may not always win, but what is important is the enjoyment of the game. Don't feel upset if it doesn't work out exactly as you'd hoped – there is always a next time. This attitude is what distinguishes the winners from the losers in life. Winners enjoy playing the game, and do not get too upset when they lose because there is always another game to be played tomorrow, and they expect to win tomorrow. When you enjoy something you relax, and that's when your abilities are most likely to shine through because you've released yourself from fear.

- **Discover your potential:** Think of all the difficulties and problems you encounter as a means to discovering your capabilities and creativity – your resourcefulness and your full potential. These challenges stretch us, and it is only when we are stretched that we discover what we can be and do. If we are not challenged by life we may never know how much we have to offer – the extent of our ability and the potentialities lying dormant within us. Just develop the attitude that you don't have a problem: you have a challenge and an opportunity.

- **Choose the best approach:** The Chinese hieroglyph, or symbol, for crisis has two meanings: 'danger' and 'opportunity'. Here is great wisdom; you can perceive the crisis, or problem, as a danger, and consequently panic or feel overwhelmed and unable to cope; or you can see the crisis as an opportunity to use your ingenuity and to demonstrate your creativity and your ability to overcome difficulties. It is your choice; which one will you choose? We know which one the successful person would choose.

Commitment

Leaders in life do not simply go to work to do their job, or to earn their pay packet. They engage in whatever they do because of a commitment to a vision, a belief or a personal philosophy. It is a commitment to a higher ideal than merely earning one's living, and the vision or philosophy generally pervades the whole of that person's life, not just their work life. There are many examples of this attitude. One that immediately springs to mind is that of the pioneering car manufacturer Henry Ford, who had a vision of providing motor cars for all ordinary people and a strong belief that it could be done. He worked tirelessly and successfully at realising the vision. Steve Jobs and Bill Gates are two more successful people who had that commitment to their vision, and in a different arena is Nelson Mandela, who never gave up his commitment to his vision of equality between races, even in terrible circumstances. The same, of course, can be said of Gandhi, Mother Teresa of Calcutta, Marie Curie, Florence Nightingale or Albert Schweitzer, and on and on; I'm sure you can think of many other examples.

- **Commit to a vision:** The list of well-known people is huge, but there are many unknown, and yet successful presidents, managing directors and CEOs of organisations, who have a vision for their particular company and what it stands for in the world. It is this kind of commitment that creates a company's culture; and just as organisations with a strong belief system or sense of mission running through them are generally more successful than ones that have no vision holding them together, the same is true for individuals. This sort of commitment fires and motivates people, giving them a purpose above and beyond mere survival, or even profit margins.

- **Stick with it:** In a committed state of mind, with a vision and a purpose, one is not easily discouraged, and this certainty of commitment provides stability in a person's life, which is very calming. An unshakable belief keeps you on course when upsets occur and life becomes turbulent. When you have this sense of commitment to whatever it is that you are working at – whether it is your career, your marriage, your local Scout group, campaigning for the environment or bringing up your children – it feels less of a chore, and more like a reason for living.

- **Define your motivations:** Try to develop a sense of commitment towards whatever you are engaged with. Try to find a purpose in what you do. I always say to my clients: 'Whatever you do, know why you're doing it.' Knowing why you are doing something is very important because it gives a sense of meaning to what you do. But also, even if it turns out to be a failure, you'll at least know why you attempted it, and that means you're in control. You can then pick yourself up and try again.

This well-known quote from Goethe emphasises the point:

'....until one is committed there is hesitancy, the chance to draw back, always ineffectiveness, concerning all acts of initiative and creation. There is one elementary truth, the ignorance of which kills countless ideas and splendid plans: that the moment one definitely commits oneself then Providence moves too. All sorts of things occur to help one that would never otherwise have occurred. A whole stream of events issues from the decision, raising in one's favour all manner of unforeseen incidents and meetings and material assistance which no man could have dreamed would have come his way. Whatever you can do, or dream you can, begin it. Boldness has genius, power and magic in it. Begin it now!'

To be successful, you have to commit yourself; otherwise, as the quote says, you will always be able to pull back. To be committed means you put all of yourself into something – it's the opposite of half-hearted.

Approaches to life

Most successful people are usually successful at a number of things; they seem to nurture and develop their different abilities and do not stagnate; they instinctively create balance in their lives. Many examples come to mind. Winston Churchill loved to paint as an antidote to his stressful career. Richard Branson engages in perilous ballooning projects – a stark contrast to sitting in an office running a business empire. Renowned English gardener Alan Titchmarsh is also a successful author of children's stories. The impressionist painter Claude Monet created an exquisite garden, which he declared was his most beautiful masterpiece, and an eminent doctor I know finds relaxation in upholstering furniture in his spare time. Many entertainers are fanatical golfers, seriously intent on perfecting their game, whilst others are excellent cooks.

How we balance our lives is always significant, and if things are swinging out of control, or we feel strained, stressed or distressed, the cause can often be traced back to a lack of the necessary balance. We have to balance 'doing' and 'being', but it's also important not to spend too much of our time focused on just one aspect of life. Many people who come to consult with me are too focused on their work. They are only using one part of themselves, usually their logical mind, and need to give expression to their other sides and their unused talents.

Is this what is happening in your life? If so, try to get back in touch with the activities you enjoyed as a child, and perhaps re-awaken your artistic or sporting abilities as a balance and counterpoint to your work life. Join a painting class, learn to sculpt or take up pottery, join your church choir, improve your tennis or golf skills or go for countryside hikes with a ramblers group, join an amateur dramatic society or a yoga or tai chi class, or learn dressmaking, millinery or a musical instrument. 'Variety is the spice of life', they say, and a variety of activities will enliven you and prevent the sort of exhaustion that arises from endless repetition of the same tasks, being focused too much, and for too long, on just one aspect of life.

Attitude

Research studies have shown that successful people almost always have an attitude in common: one that is a decidedly positive, upbeat attitude. One in-depth study by the University of California, on happiness in particular, found that a positive, 'can do' approach was not the result of achieving success, but that the attitude was there first, before the achievement. A positive, or happy, attitude is not necessarily something you are born with; you can train yourself to be more positive in your approach to everything you are dealing with. You just have to believe that thinking positively will help and empower you, and recognise that dwelling on problems doesn't get you anywhere. Then find ways to make sure that you emphasise the positive aspects, and limit the amount of time you spend focusing on the negatives of any situation. Think of how athletes, for example, talk about their performances – always with an upbeat attitude, never for a moment discussing the possibility of failure. Successful people expect to be successful and never dwell on past failures or mistakes, except possibly to learn the lesson. Conversely, unsuccessful people tend to re-play their past failures over and over in their minds, instead of just letting them go, and moving on. A positive attitude to failure is summed up in the words of Henry Ford: 'Failure is simply the opportunity to begin again more intelligently.'

In a recent radio interview, a well-known explorer was talking about his expedition to the Antarctic, and one of the things he said about survival in extreme conditions could also be a guiding principle for approaching the difficulties of everyday life. He said: 'You must develop the attitude of mind of making the snow and ice your friend and not your enemy.' He knew the importance of one's inner attitude for a successful outcome. In those treacherous conditions the help from inside themselves, in the absence of other sources, is vital. This is a tremendously important lesson for life: whatever you have to deal with – be it a traffic jam, a report you have to write, a presentation you have to give at work, a TV interview, an exam or even incessant questions from your kids – if you can make it your friend instead of your enemy, you will relax and feel harmonious, and use far less effort than if you are gearing up for a fight. Think about how your body posture changes when you are about to greet a friend: you anticipate pleasure and ease, so you relax and open up to enjoyment and fun. Try to see the tasks of your day as friends and fun.

We so often stress ourselves by thinking negatively about whatever is facing us: seeing it as a trap, or an enemy that is out to get us, to harm us or bring us down. But something is only what we *think* it is; if we don't think it's a problem then it won't be, so it is really very important to work at this. Negativity is extremely disempowering, it saps your energy.

Be yourself!

Top people are usually true to themselves, value self-expression and have the courage to be who they are rather than being hung-up on the need to please others. This is very empowering. However, it is not usually until mid-life that anyone begins to know who they truly are; before this we are generally experimenting with different personas, and trying out different ways of behaving to get what we want. It is also difficult to throw off the conditioning of your upbringing and your parents' voices about what is, or is not, acceptable. But try to listen to the inner voice, or inner feeling, that knows when you are being true or false to yourself.

I was recently asked: 'What in your experience do you consider is the one most important thing to aim for in order to be happy and fulfilled?' My unhesitating reply was: 'Be yourself'. It can be very difficult to be yourself, but at least try to be 'authentic' or 'real'. Have you noticed how the truly great men and women usually have an air of authenticity about them? It is a sign of being at peace with yourself – not smug and self-satisfied, but accepting of who you are. So, work at being 'yourself' as much as you can. You were born to be you.

I read a very amusing quote recently, supposedly from Charles Schulz, the creator of the comic strip 'Peanuts'. It said: 'Be yourself, everyone else is taken!' Wisdom indeed: you might like to write that down and carry it around with you.

Another inspiring quote from the psychoanalyst Carl Jung says: 'You do not have to become perfect, all you have to do is become who you have always been.' You are unique, and have unique gifts to offer the world. No-one else can do it exactly like you; so honour yourself. It may take a long time to know who you have always been, but keep trying to be the authentic person that is you, and only you. You were not meant to be anyone else.

This really is the greatest goal to aim for, and my suggestions throughout this book are intended to assist you towards becoming more authentically 'you', and to free you from the constraints that stress you and that get in the way of being peacefully yourself. It is a journey that may take a while, but just enjoy the fun and the challenge as you work at creating a fulfilling life with a high degree of stress control.

Afterword

I have presented you with my ideas and suggestions as well as the essential information to help and guide you to feeling more in control of the stresses in your life. I hope I have shown you that stress control is often achieved by taking a different view of things, by changing your perspective and the way you approach the demands you face. This is a major key to controlling your stress and your life. Everything can be experienced from a number of different standpoints, and it is important to remember this; just because you have always seen something one way does not mean that there is no other way to view it, or that you have to see it as you have always done. We usually have more choices than we imagine, and so keep asking yourself: 'Is there another way I could be looking at this?' In this way you can transform difficulties and move forwards, because you increase your options. However, there may be times when you need help to see things more clearly, so never be afraid to seek help or advice from people in the caring professions – especially from specialist counsellors, or your doctor, who are specifically trained and have experience in helping and advising people with similar problems and dilemmas. (See Useful Addresses for counselling organisations.)

Most importantly, please remember that it takes time to bring about changes in ourselves and in our outlook. Be patient and gentle with yourself. If one day it isn't working and you feel downhearted or overwhelmed just reassure yourself, encourage yourself that tomorrow it can all be different. Each day is a new opportunity to get it right, to make things work better, to make your life more beautiful. Say to yourself: 'What a difference a day makes'; the days of our lives are like the weather, ever changing. Just because today may be stormy, or dull and heavy, it doesn't mean that tomorrow will be exactly the same. The bad times roll away like the dark clouds and suddenly, unexpectedly, the sun bursts through, or a solution presents itself. So never despair. Especially never forget that the sun is always there, it doesn't disappear – it just gets covered up, or escapes our gaze for a while, but it still exists somewhere. This is what happens to the good things in life. They may sometimes get covered up, but they are always there, waiting for us to find our way back to them. I hope this book has shown you some of the ways back – back to how you want it to be, ways to make your life less stressful and more harmonious, happy and relaxed.

Your helplist

Cut this out to carry around with you as a helpful reminder!

1. Keep a constant check on the number of changes you are dealing with, and avoid making any unnecessary changes when you are stressed. Too much change at any one time will overload your coping ability.
2. Balance tension and relaxation: doing and non-doing. Take the pressure off yourself regularly.
3. Use the Relaxation Response more often than the Stress Response. Learn to switch off the Fight or Flight reaction – it winds you up and wears you out.
4. Manage your boundaries. Give yourself permission to say 'No' or 'Not now'. Practice the Positive 'No'.
5. Take good care of yourself: exercise your body, inspire your mind and protect your emotions. Acknowledge your needs: give to yourself so that you can give to others.
6. Nurture your relationships. Develop supportive networks. Take time off from your problems and seek out the people who care for you and give you positive feedback about yourself.
7. Acknowledge your personal truths and seek inspiration in the wise teachings of the past. Hold onto whatever you find valuable from the past whilst embracing the new. Do it your way.
8. Eat well to support yourself. Remember that food and drink are the raw materials your body uses to renew itself.

9. Think positively. Visualise what you want to make happen and how you want your life to be. Fill your mind with positive images.

10. Create a healthy, positive and beautiful environment at home and in your office, or wherever you work.

11. Remember the secrets of successful people, the three Cs: control, challenge, commitment. The more you feel in control the less you will feel stressed. Most importantly, you can always have control of yourself and your reactions. See problems as challenges to your ingenuity and creativity, not as threats. Make a total commitment to whatever you engage in; find a higher purpose or an altruistic reason for your endeavours and you will remove the strain.

12. When things seem at their worst, or when you feel most stress, rise above it! Practise becoming still and connecting with the peace and silence that lie behind the noise and rush. Regularly practise deep relaxation. Be in the NOW moment.

13. Remember: love changes everything. Practice love. Above all, love yourself.

Useful addresses

Relaxometers and biofeedback machines

Aleph One Ltd.
The Old Courthouse, 123 High Street, Bottisham, Cambridge CB25 9BA
Tel: +44 (0)1223 811 679
Email: info@aleph1.co.uk URL: www.aleph1.co.uk/bio
Also: books and CDs on stress management, relaxation, behavioural problems and anxiety.

Biofeedback equipment

Relax UK Ltd.
Tel: +44 (0)1206 767300
Email: info@relax-uk.com URL: www.relax-uk.com

Acoustic screens and office furniture, including fully adjustable chairs

Inter County
17-20 Greenfield, Royston, Hertfordshire SG8 5HN
Tel: 0845 095 1122
Email: sales@intercounty.com URL: www.intercounty.com

Posture cushions, ergonomic furniture, document holders, foot rests, posture advice, workstation assessment and set-up

Posturite (UK) Ltd.
Tel: 0845 345 0010
Email: sales@posturite.co.uk URL: www.posturite.co.uk

Full spectrum light bulbs and Light Boxes for SAD (Seasonal Affective Disorder)

Full Spectrum Lighting Ltd.
Trading as S.A.D. Lightbox Company
Unit 2, Aston Hill, Lewknor, Watlington, Oxon OX49 5SG
Tel: 0845 095 6477 International tel: +44 1844 353 136
Email: customerservice@sad.uk.com URL: www.sad.uk.com

Full Spectrum Tubes

www.GBBulbs.co.uk

Light Boxes

www.electronichealing.co.uk

www.amnestyshop.org.uk/Biobulbs
Full spectrum bulbs that use 75% less energy than standard light bulbs.

www.amazon.co.uk
Full spectrum light bulbs and SAD products.

Information and advice on SAD

URL: www.sad.org.uk
Gives in-depth information on SAD and lists recommended manufacturers of Light Boxes who are supported by genuine medical research and registered with the Medical Devices Agency. Also supplies information on White Light and Blue Light boxes, and Dawn Simulators.

The Seasonal Affective Disorder Association
SAD Association, PO Box 989, Steyning, Sussex BN44 3HG
URL: www.sada.org.uk

Voluntary organisation and registered charity offering support, information and advice. Also supplies hire prices for Light Boxes. Send SAE for information by post.

Air Ionisers

URL: www.amazinghealth.co.uk
Tel: 0845 838 6162/6263
Also sells Himalayan natural salt lamps that ionise the atmosphere and neutralise electro-smog build-up from computers, printers, TVs and other electrical devices.

www.amazon.co.uk
Supplies a range of different-sized negative ionisers.

Also:
www.bodykind.com Call free on: 0800 043 5566
www.AllergyMatters.com

Tai Chi information

International Directory for Tai Chi and related exercises/martial arts
URL: www.taichifinder.co.uk
Tai Chi Union for Great Britain (has international list of over 800 Tai Chi instructors)
Contact: Peter Ballam (Secretary), 5 Corunna Drive, Horsham, West Sussex RH13 5HG
Tel: +44 (0)1403 257 918
URL: www.taichiunion.com

Learn Tai Chi online:
URL: www.GetTaiChiOnline.com

Easy Tai Chi DVDs:
URL: www.easyTaiChi.com

Yoga, meditation and mindfulness

Yoga classes in London (including classes for kids) for all levels of ability. Also classes on meditation, positive thinking and developing willpower. Courses and Retreats in France, Austria and India. The Sivananda Yoga Vedanta Centre, 45–51 Felsham Road, Putney, London SW15 1AZ
Tel: +44 (0)20 8780 0160
Email: London@sivananda.net URL: www.sivananda.co.uk
or www.sivananda.eu

British Wheel of Yoga
For full information pack:
BWY Central Office, British Wheel of Yoga, 25 Jermyn Street, Sleaford, Lincolnshire NG34 7RU
Send SAE for details of yoga courses throughout the UK.
Tel: +44 (0)1529 306851
Email: office@bwy.org.uk URL: www.bwy.org.uk

Iyengar Yoga Association
www.iyengaryoga.org.uk

The School of Meditation
158 Holland Park Avenue, London W11 4UH
Tel: +44 (0)20 7603 6116
Email: info@schoolofmeditation.org URL: www.schoolofmeditation.org
Groups in Holland and Greece as well as the UK.

Free lessons online + CDs and books
www.learnmindfulness.co.uk
Tel: +44 (0)20 7060 3392 and mobile: 07903 343 893 for free conversation
Email: shamash@learnmindfulness.co.uk

Mindfulness based Stress Reduction at:
London Shambhala Meditation Centre
27 Belmont Close, London SW4 6AY
Tel: +44 (0)20 7720 3207
URL: www.shambhala.org

Also:
www.londonmeditationcentre.com (with links to New York Meditation Centre and Retreats in India)
www.london–meditation.co.uk

Retreats for relaxation, rejuvenation, yoga, meditation and Ayurveda therapies

Samye Ling Retreat
A peaceful Tibetan Buddhist centre offering meditation classes and retreats, open to people of all faiths and none.
Eskdalemuir, Langholm, Dumfriesshire DG13 OQL Scotland
Tel: 013873 73232
URL: www.samyeling.org
See their website for details of Samye Ling's association with Aberdeen University's programme in Mindfulness studies.

Swaswara
Om Beach, Donibhail, Gokarna, Uttara Kannada, Karnataka – 581326, India
Tel: 08386 257132/33/235197
Email: swaswara@cghearth.com URL: www.swaswara.com
A sanctuary situated on the west coast of India, south of Goa. In Sanskrit 'swa' means 'the self' and 'swara' implies 'sound'. Here the aim is to discover the sound of your inner self with yoga, meditation, Ayurveda therapies, organic holistic cuisine, amid beautiful, natural surroundings.

Also: for other retreat sanctuaries of CGH Earth go to: www.cg-hearth.com

Jnane Tamsna
Douar Abiad, La Palmeraie, 40000 Marrakech, Morocco
Tel: +212 524 32 84 84
Email: meryanne@jnane.com URL: www.jnane.com
A haven of peace in which to relax and restore yourself.

Happiness and Laughter Clubs

The Happiness Project of Dr. Robert Holden
Tel: 0845 430 9236
Email: info@happiness.co.uk
URL: www.happiness.co.uk

Laughter Yoga International
#22, Sri Balaji Pride, Flat No.F-2, 5th Cross, Bendre Nagar, Bangalore – 560 070, India
Tel: +91-80-26660284
Email: info@laughteryoga.org URL: http://laughteryoga.org
For information on 6000 laughter yoga clubs in over 60 countries.

Also: For laughter yoga teacher training and workshops.
Tel: + 44 (0) 844 335 1552
Email: info@unitedmind.co.uk URL: www.unitedmind.co.uk

www.totallylaughteryoga.co.uk
Email: totallylaughteryoga@yahoo.co.uk
Tel: + 44 (0) 7843 106 127

Relaxation and stress management

International Stress Management Association
PO Box 491, Bradley Stoke, Bristol BS34 9AH
Tel: +44 (0) 1179 697284
URL: www.isma.org.uk

Stress Management Society
Tel: + 44 (0) 800 327 7697 & + 44 (0) 203 142 8650
Email: info@stress.org.uk URL: www.stress.org.uk

Stresswise
Tel: +44 (0) 845 0568977
URL: www.stresswise.com

Relaxation for Living & More,
32 Cottenham Park Road, London SW20 0SA
Tel: 0333 700 4277 or mobile: 07962 811 990
Email: info@rfli.co.uk URL: www.rfli.co.uk

Counselling, psychotherapy and complementary therapies

The Hale Clinic
7 Park Crescent, London W1B 1PF
Tel: + 44 (0) 20 7631 0156
URL: www.haleclinic.com
Europe's largest complementary health clinic offering a wide range of holistic therapies. There are over 80 therapists specialising in various disciplines. Several practitioners are medical physicians and many are multi-disciplinary.

Cruse Bereavement Care
PO Box 800, Richmond, Surrey TW9 1RG
Daytime Helpline: 0844 477 9400 Scotland Tel: 0845 600 2227
Free daytime phone helpline for young people: 0808 808 1677
Email: helpline@cruse.org.uk
URL: www.crusebereavementcare.org.uk
For Scotland: www.crusescotland.org.uk
For young people: www.rd4u.org.uk. See website for all types of bereavement counselling.

Westminster Pastoral Foundation
23 Magdalen Street, London SE1 2EN
Tel: +44 (0) 20 7378 2000
Email: reception@wpf.org.uk URL: www.wpf.org.uk
A charity offering counselling for a range of problems such as: phobias, anxiety, trauma, post-traumatic stress disorder or addictions for individuals and couples. WPF operates a sliding scale of fees to make therapy affordable for everyone.

To search for a counsellor or psychotherapist near you visit: www.counselling-directory.org.uk

Or contact: British Association for Counselling and Psychotherapy (BACP)
Tel: 01455 883300
Email: bacp@bacp.co.uk URL: www.bacp.co.uk
For a nationwide list of qualified practitioners.

Positive Performance Coaching
Wendy Chalmers Mill's company in Stirlingshire, Scotland, offers: ergonomics expert advice, corporate coaching and NLP training.
Tel: 01786 818788 (mobile: 07973 262005).
Email: info@positive-performance.com
URL: www.positive-performance.com

Also:
UK Council for Psychotherapy (UKCP)
Tel: + 44 (0) 20 7014 9955
Email: info@ukcp.org.uk URL: www.psychotherapy.org.uk
For a national register of qualified psychotherapists and psychotherapeutic counsellors.

For relationship problems, marriage guidance, family counselling and counselling for children:

Relate
Tel: 0300 100 1234 Scotland Tel: 0845 119 2020
URL: www.relate.org.uk For Scotland: www.relationships-scotland.org.uk.

Family Lives
A national charity offering advice and support in all aspects of family life. You can live-chat 7 days a week with a trained support worker on Freephone: 0808 800 2222.
Email: parentsupport@familylives.org.uk
URL: www.familylives.org.uk

Nutrition

The Institute for Optimum Nutrition
Avalon House, 72 Lower Mortlake Road, Richmond TW9 2JY
Tel: + 44 (0) 20 8614 7800
Email: ionclinic@ion.ac.uk URL: www.ion.ac.uk
Provides nutrition therapy education.

Food Standards Agency
An independent government department set up to protect the public's health and regulate the food industry. Provide up-to-date details of allergy alerts, nutrition labelling, and government guideline recommendations on nutrition.
Tel: + 44 (0) 20 7276 8829
Email: helpline@foodstandards.gsi.gov.uk
URL: www.food.gov.uk

The Nutri Centre
7 Park Crescent, London W1B 1PF
Tel: + 44 (0) 20 7436 5122
For orders: +44 (0) 20 8752 8450
Email: admin@nutricentre.com URL: www.nutricentre.com
Located on the lower ground floor of the Hale Clinic, this renowned centre provides a vast range of nutritional supplements and holistic remedies, with a natural medicines dispensary and advice from qualified practitioners in nutritional and complementary medicine. They provide a dedicated nutrition helpline and an international delivery service. There is also a library and bookshop supplying books on complementary and holistic treatments and therapies and meditation CDs. See their website for details of their other stores around the UK.

The Herb Society
Sulgrave Manor, PO Box 946, Northampton NN3 0BN
Tel: + 44 (0) 845 491 8699
Email: info@herbsociety.org.uk URL: www.herbsociety.org.uk
The UK's leading society for increasing understanding, use and appreciation of herbs and their benefits to health.

National Institute of Medical Herbalists
Tel: + 44 (0) 1392 426 022
Email: info@nimh.org.uk URL: www.nimh.org.uk
Provides a register of qualified medical herbalists.

Slow Food International
Slow Food is a non-profit, eco-gastronomic member-supported organisation, founded in 1989 to counteract fast food and fast life. It has a network of 100,000 members in 153 countries, promoting good, clean and fair food for all. Slow Food encourages and supports nutritious food production and consumption that does

not harm the environment, animal welfare or our health, and that is fairly priced for consumers and farmers.
URL: www.slowfood.com

The George Mateljan Foundation for the World's Healthiest Foods
This online site provides in-depth, scientifically proven, clear and easy to understand nutritional information on how to eat for maximum health and wellbeing. Also offers excellent recipes, cooking methods and menu plans for the healthiest way of eating.
URL: www.whfoods.org

Get away from it all

Jonathan's Tours: guided walking holidays in mainland Greece, the Greek islands, the French and Spanish Pyrenees, and Morocco. The Moroccan walking tours are new, and part of the payment for these is donated to initiatives educating children, courses for farmers and other community projects in Morocco. Jonathan Peat, who leads the walking tours, is a qualified European Mountain Leader. He lives in South West France, in the Ariege district close to the Pyrenees. He and his wife, Myriam, speak fluent Greek, French and English.
Tel & Fax: 00 33 561046447 (mobile: 0033 673707804).
Email: myriam.peat@wanadoo.fr. Or jonathanstours@gmail.com
URL: www.jonathanstours.com

Nordic Walking. This is an enhancement of ordinary walking, using poles to walk more strenuously and to utilise the muscles in the upper body as well as the lower body.
Tel: 0845 260 9339. Email: info@nordicwalking.co.uk
URL: www.nordicwalking.co.uk

The Ramblers. A British registered charity that promotes rambling, protects rights of way, campaigns for access to open country and defends the countryside.

For general enquiries: Tel: + 44 (0)20 7339 8500.

Fax: 020 7339 8501.

Email: ramblers@ramblers.org.uk URL: www.ramblers.org.uk

Suggested further reading

Campbell, T. Colin and Campbell, Thomas M., *The China Study*, BenBella Books, 2006

Chopra, Deepak, *Ageless Body, Timeless Mind*, Rider, 2008

Covey, Stephen R., *The Seven Habits of Highly Effective People*, Simon & Schuster, first published 1989, new edition 2004

Dalai Lama and Cutler, Howard C., *The Art of Happiness in a Troubled World*, Hodder & Stoughton, 2009

Dalai Lama and Norman, Alexander, *Ancient Wisdom, Modern World: Ethics for the New Millennium*, Abacus, 2000, reprinted 2001, 2002, 2003

Diamond, Harvey and Diamond, Marilyn, *Fit For Life*, Bantam, 1995

Ferris, Tim, *The 4-Hour Week*, Vermillion, 2011

Frankl, Viktor, *Man's Search for Meaning*, Rider, 2004

Gilbert, Paul, *The Compassionate Mind*, Constable, 2010

Grant, Doris, *Food Combining for Life*, Thorsons, 1995

Hendrix, Harville, *Getting the Love You Want*, Pocket Books, an imprint of Simon & Schuster, 2005

Jeffers, Susan, *End the Struggle and Dance with Life*, Hodder & Stoughton, 1996

Jeffers, Susan, *Feel the Fear and Do It Anyway*, revised and updated edition by Vermillion, an imprint of Ebury Press, Random House, 2007

Kabat-Zinn, Jon, *Wherever You Go, There You Are: Mindfulness Meditation for Everyday Life*, Piatkus Books, 2004

Rowe, Dorothy, *Depression: The Way Out of Your Prison*, Routledge, third edition 2003

Sigman, Aric, *Remotely Controlled: How Television is Damaging Our Lives*, Vermillion, 2007

Tissier, Jackie le, *Food Combining for Vegetarians*, Thorsons, 1992

Tolle, Eckhart, *The Power of Now*, Hodder & Stoughton, 1999, 2005, 2011

Trickett, Shirley, *Coping Successfully with Panic Attacks*, Sheldon Press, 1998

Weekes, Claire, *Self Help for Your Nerves*, Thorsons, 1995

Young, Robert O., and Young, Shelley Redford, *The pH Miracle: Balance Your Diet, Reclaim Your Health*, Piatkus, 2009, 2010, 2011

Recommended 'Little' Books

Dalai Lama, *The Dalai Lama's Book of Wisdom*, Thorsons, an imprint of HarperCollins, 2012

Gibran, Kahlil, *The Prophet*, Heinemann, 1993

Jeffers, Susan, *The Little Book of Confidence*, Rider, an imprint of Ebury Publishing, Random House, 1999

Pas, Julian F., *The Wisdom of the Tao*, Oneworld Publications, 2000

Too, Lillian, *Little Book of Feng Shui at Work*, Element, 1999

White Eagle, *The Quiet Mind*, The White Eagle Publishing Trust, 1998

Wilson, Paul, *The Little Book of Calm*, Penguin Books, 1997

Wilson, Paul, *The Little Book of Hope*, Penguin Books, 1999

Index

This book must be returned on or before
the date last stamped below, unless it
is previously recalled by the Library.

Fines are incurred on overdue books
(See Library Regulations)